Voyage in France by a Frenchman

Paul Verlaine

Translated By Richard Robinson

Sunny Lou Publishing Company
Portland, Oregon, USA
http://www.sunnyloupublishing.com

2nd Edition: June 1, 2024

Original Publication Date: November 10, 2021

ISBN: 978-1-955392-70-9

# # #

This translation from French is based on the
Librairie Léon Vanier, Publisher, 2nd edition of
Voyage en France par un Français, Paris, 1907.

Contents

Foreword by the Translator

This literary curiosity and polemic by Paul Verlaine may surprise those readers of his who are familiar with his work but used to something a little more, how should I call it, peppery? – more liberal, assuredly, and decidedly decadent. I don't say "more decadent" because this piece is not decadent at all, quite the opposite. But decadence – that's what we know and that's what we love about Paul Verlaine, isn't that right?

Indeed, if there was one poet or writer in all of 19th-century French literature who deserved the moniker *decadent* more than any other (except maybe Rimbaud), it would have to be Paul Verlaine. And I would bet my wages for a week, to the first ten unary people that stumbled along, that 9 out of 10 of them would say the same thing: Paul Verlaine. Paul Verlaine is the decadent poet *par excellence* of 19th-century France. For all the reasons you know. (And if you don't know read *My Prisons*.)

But *Voyage in France by a Frenchman* is not that kind of work, and not that kind of Verlaine, not the Verlaine you expect. It reads more like something Léon Bloy might have written than our Poor Lélian. The vocabulary is Bloyian; the long, periodic sentences with multiple interjections, parentheses, asides, etc, are Bloyian. The conservative and Catholic point of view is Bloyian. How in God's bountiful universe is that even possible? What in the world gives?

What gives is that Verlaine wrote this piece in that fecund period of his life when he was again, and still, a Catholic – some time after that famous conversion to Catholicism of his that happened in Mons Prison, where he wrote some of the best poetry of his career: *Cellulely* (*Cellulairement* in French) contains the lion's share of the poems written in captivity, which later made it into *Sagesse, Jadis et Naguère*, and *Parallèlement,* accordingly. *Cellulely* as a collection of poetry is interesting in that it shows Verlaine writing poems of two very different styles: the style we love, and a different (but not new) style, that we may not. It is in light of that different style, and of that also Catholic poetry that one should read *this* work. I don't say, or even suggest, that this other style is not a good style; on the contrary, it is an excellent style and I love it a bunch. I am merely saying that it is different, different from what I myself expected, different from what you probably expect, in the same way as some poems in *Cellulely* are different from those in *Romances sans paroles* or, say, *Poèmes saturniens* (but like the first of that book). It's not because they are Catholic (though they are), it's not because they are conservative and reactionary (though they are), it's not because they employ an entirely different style and diction (though they do), it's not that they are not nuanced (they are not, or not in the same way)... What is the word that I'm looking for here... sober. This work, like *those* poems in *Cellulely* that you didn't expect to read, – they are sober.

But back to Bloy for a moment. The two of

them, Verlaine and Bloy, knew each other personally – I wouldn't say *well*, and certainly not in the same way Verlaine knew Rimbaud – but they (Bloy and Verlaine) crossed paths more than once in life, during the Belle Epoque, in the early days of the *Chat Noir* cabaret and journal. Let's hear what Verlaine has to say about an encounter he had with Bloy, as recorded in *Mes Prisons*:

> *Now, from the old* Chat Noir, *today the* Mirliton, *– transitions! – I exited, one early evening, leaving behind me the delightful Salis[1] and the then* persona grata *Léon Bloy, tiger of the good God, and cat of the good devil, and Marie Krysinka, and so many other lovable monsters, after several extremely prolonged libations? no! well maybe.*
>
> *I left them then these delightful individuals, and I wended, living in the vicinity of the Bastille, past a station of fiacres not far away, in order to return to my, as yet filial, domicile...*
>
> *But what the devil got into me? I wanted to refresh the other drinks with ONE last absinthe.*
>
> *An error in the accounting, after a series of absorptions, caused an outburst, and I felt the need to demand – a lot and very loudly! – my rights.*

[1]Salis: Rodolphe Salis, founder of the Chat Noir, a celebrated cabaret in Montmartre. See *Ten Years a Bohemian* by Emile Goudeau for a story of its beginnings.

As it turns out, he ended up in jail that night, to sleep it off. So much for a "refresher." (I read somewhere, I can't remember where, by someone, I can't remember whom, that Bloy and Verlaine once went to fisticuffs. Perhaps it was on this occasion.)

I don't know about you, but when I read the chapter "To My Son" in this book by Verlaine, and knowing what I know about Verlaine and his drinking habits and his history, I feel that the advice he gives his son about not drinking, – must come directly from his own experience. That sounds supererogatory to say. But he sounds convincing. He is convincing. He knows what he is talking about when it comes to the sins and seductions of the harmless "drop," one drop after the next, until...

But the above reference to Bloy (o! only in passing) is about all I can remember of Verlaine mentioning him in his work.

Bloy, on the other hand, mentions Verlaine rather often, if also only in passing, but often enough, over the course of the years, in various works of his, making it clear that he had a long-lasting, steady, and high appreciation of him as a poet, not as a man, but as a poet, and particularly as a Catholic poet.

In fact, it was on reading *She Who Weeps* recently that I first learnt about the existence of this posthumous work by Verlaine that you hold in your hands. Here is what Bloy says there:

> *Once again, I have not undertaken to*
> *explain those deep and divine similari-*

ties, nor even to show them, for the intended execution of which more light is needed, I suppose, than God habitually accords writers who are not ecclesiastical writers. But consider this, much to the point, a small and very posthumous book by Paul Verlaine, Voyage in France by a Frenchman, *which contains a nice protestation by that great unfortunate poet against work on Sunday.*

Ah! I am fully aware that he is not, he neither, an authority. Far from it! One will realize eventually, in the pious world, that Paul Verlaine wrote the most beautiful Catholic verse there is, in praise of "his Mother Mary," to the glory of Penance and the Holy Sacrament, and that he is, in reality, the only Catholic poet since the inspired ones of the great Hymnary; but it will take time. Another half a century for the elite among our seminaries, and one hundred years at least for one third of the others, from the time of François Coppée's death, which does not appear impending. All the same, "poor Lélian," towards 1880, presented in prose that original and great idea that the law of work, ordinarily regarded as a malediction, is, on the contrary, the "last and only consoling memory of earthly Paradise." On reading that, I believe I have seen the so-well guarded Gate open up before me just a crack.

> *Ah! how fine that is! Thus God, totally upset as he is against man and condemning him to lose everything, would have employed this adorable ruse to flagellate with Hope, to inflict on him like a chastisement what ought to be his recomfort and to tie him up rudely by a chain of Dilection! Caught up in his own, much stronger, foot-locks, the lamentable Verlaine – he saw that! He saw, or he saw briefly, that if a lazy man effected the terrify-ing act of severing the last mooring rope, that perverse worker, who is only courageous on Sundays because he can brave an invisible master, – he renews, unbeknownst to himself, being a frightening beast, the original Crime and loses again the Garden of Volup-tuousness, every time, for himself and for many others.*

Voyage in France by a Frenchman is a con-servative work then. It is a sober work. It is a piece of work written by the Catholic Verlaine, very different in tone, style, subject matter, and point of view from anything the decadent Verlaine might have written.

Verlaine was a complicated man. He was more than the sum of his very different, sometimes opposing and sometimes even contradictory, parts:

Catholic, not Catholic; decadent, not decadent; sober, drunk... – which one is the true Verlaine? Neither, or both. But certainly not one or the other. Complicated as he was, like all geniuses are – it's important that certain groups today (and yesterday and tomorrow) don't try to co-opt him or claim him for their own, to the exclusion of others. (You know who you are, you know when you are called out.) Verlaine would no more approve of that than he would approve of his being called a bohemian. He was no more decadent than he was Catholic. Or no less. He was, well, frankly, just being himself, always and ever, awful and glorious as the case might be. For lack of a better word, I'd like to think of him as unary, which may sound surprising. In large part, because it does not mean all that much. And whatever it does mean, to me, it probably does not mean the same thing to you. Which is good. He was unary, then, amidst the many. Maybe we should leave him that way. Isn't that right?

– Richard Robinson, November 10, 2021

Original Preface

Voyage in France by a Frenchman has remained unknown to Verlaine biographers; the title itself can be
found mentioned only on the liminary page of the
first edition of *Sagesse*, published by Palmé, in 1881.

It seems surprising that Poor Lélian, always
without two nickles to rub together, should have held
on to the pages of a piece of writing without trying to
draw some profit from them. However, *Voyage in
France* followed the adventurous career of the poet
for ten years without his being able to find a publisher
for it. No one, apparently, was seduced by this violent, reactionary pamphlet elaborated around 1880,
during the time of mystical renaissance in which were
composed the verses of sweet piety comprising the
collection *Sagesse*, which *Voyage in France* is the
virulent paraphrase of. The manuscript, ready for the
printer, written on poor-quality school paper, must
have been reserved for a better occasion.

In the month of July, 1891, that occasion presented itself under rather original circumstances.

At that time, Verlaine, at the end of his resources, was
two hundred francs behind on his rent. He needed to
make money any way that he could. By a happy
chance, he succeeded in persuading his hotelier to accept, in exchange for his debt, the unpublished copy
of *Voyage of a Frenchman* which he dug up from
somewhere. A contract was drawn up, and a stamped

document recorded the following declaration:

> *I, the undersigned, declare to have sold to M. X***, a manuscript entitled "Voyage in France by a Frenchman," as well as the rights of author and of publication, for the sum of two hundred francs and give him all authorization to negotiate its sale or publication as he sees fit.*
>
> *Paris, the twentieth of July one thousand eight hundred ninety-one.*
>
> *– Paul Verlaine, Paris, 18, rue Descartes.*

M. X***, delighted by the windfall, immediately went out to negotiate the publication of the volume for profit. He wanted to speculate on the famous name, but the directors of reviews, distrustful and perhaps also put off by his excessive pretensions, did not respond to his call and dismissed him. M. X*** saw his golden dreams collapse, he feared even lest the manuscript should count for nothing, when my godfather, M. Delzant, learning about his misadventure, purchased the pledge, informed the author, and placed the notebook on a privileged shelf of his library.

Today, Verlaine's polemic maintains only a retrospective interest: the prejudices against it have no longer any reason to exist. That is why I offer to the curiosity of readers these "refound pages" which merit, in my opinion, holding a place among the posthumous Works of the poet, for they offer a psychological document of the most singular kind and can serve to comment on and explain certain pages of *Sagesse* and of *Bonheur*.

Voyage in France recalls, by its general tone, the rudest articles by Veuillot whose influence can be seen on every page. This work differs essentially from what the poet has otherwise published, and can be compared only with *Invectives*, – a collection of verse that contains moreover two pieces (*Buste pour mairies*, and *Nébuleuses*) written during the same period, in the same style as *Voyage*, – but it is that same curious, and so personal prose that we are already familiar with. Its periodic sentences, long and charged, demand a precise and sustained punctuation; the flow of ideas is often stopped by reticences, parentheses, parenthetical clauses. The style is that of a discourse during the coarse of which the orator would be interrupted constantly to respond to an objection or point out a stronger argument.

The first part of the work presents a somber tableau of our country. Bitter critic, Verlaine positions himself principally from the religious point of view and, with the faith of a neophyte, with the zeal of a preacher, describes the contemporary abomination, fruit of the general impiety and abandonment of ancient principles. He regrets times passed, deplores the expulsion of the Jesuits, attacks those who have struck a blow against the absolute supremacy of spiritual power,

and does not fail to make a heartfelt allusion to the
catechism of Mgr. Gaume, the which, one remem-
bers, was the principal instrument of his conversion.[2]
Then, after numerous counsels to his son on how he
should conduct himself in our times, the author
changes tack quickly and consecrates the second part
of the volume to contemporary literature and discusses novels where religion is called into question.

It is the most cut-and-dried section, the most
curious in *Voyage*; they are above all the only pages
wherein Verlaine has presented a work of open criti-
cism, for the *Poètes maudits*, and other studies published by Vanier, are not, properly speaking, but cir-
cumstantial notes. Those he praises: Barbey d'Aurevilly and Paul Féval (!) "two incontestable masters";
those he attacks: the Brothers Goncourt, Zola, Vallès,
– and the greats: Flaubert and Daudet.

As for Flaubert, Verlaine will declare that the
abbot Bournisien and the abbot Jeufroy aren't given
all desirable relief, without however his appearing to
have taken a side, Flaubert having relegated them to
the rank of vulgar "subjects"; – Zola commits monstruous errors and lets himself go with obscene fan-
tasies; – the Brothers Goncourt are disconcerting; –
Vallès has quite a few qualities, he does not practice

---

[2]Original footnote: In *Mes Prisons*, Verlaine will judge that small
volume more severely: "I'm a man of letters," he wrote, "I
appreciate correctness, subtlety, the complete cuisine of style, as
by right and duty. Even these corrections, these subtleties, I took
them, I sniffed at them, if you will. And I'm horrified by all written
platitudes. But, in spite of an actual deplorable art of writing and
syntax that had barely any life to it, Monseigneur Gaume was for
me, oozing with pride, the apostle of syntax and Parisian
stupidity."

theology, but he is absolutely mistaken when he brings priests onto the scene and gives testimony of a spirit of unsupportable insult; – as for Daudet... Verlaine is no longer a critic, but an extreme caricature, able only to make the admirers of his genius smile, without offending.

I felt the need not to omit anything from these pages, for they demonstrate in a particularly characteristic fashion that, with Verlaine, the complexity of his feeling explains sometimes the strangeness of his judgments. What's more, he admits as much himself: and to prove it, I need only cite these four lines of verse that I would be tempted to place as an epigraph to *Voyage*:

However, – and this is a case in point, – I have my practical
Moments, serious if you like, where ire,
Fundamentally just, fundamentally unjust in the worst case,
Leaves me in order to enjoy a great feast, tooth and nail.[3].

LOUIS LOVIOT

---

[3]"However... nail:" a stanza from the poem "Ad Hoc Ars Poetica" in *Invectives*.

Chapter 1: Exposé

Only the most ardent love for the fatherland could have inspired this book: one will be convinced of it on reading it. But under the current state of things, the author, preoccupied with guiding his love in the right direction, has sought two habitual objects of love, the head and the heart, and not finding the one, he would be tempted to grow saddened by his near inability to reach the other, except through his imagination, that is through his memory.

He will explain.

What one loves in a woman, for example, – it goes without saying that only the most elevated sort of love is meant here, – is beauty or, for lack of beauty, but sometimes by preference, the look on her face, intelligence, nobility, kindness, and, as it is through the eyes that the heart speaks, at the start of an affair, it is the eyes that one looks at after the first shock and *crystallization* that Stendhal speaks of. Now, present-day France has no head, and what has replaced it, depending on the body and commanded by it, is no more or less, under the same very bloody *bonnet rouge*[4] as before, and very grimy at present, than a servile, violent, and monstrous as possible confabulation of poor noggins filled with dizziness and, short of that, empty of all else. How to try and love that hydra and to find, in those five hundred and some odd pairs

---

[4] *bonnet rouge*: French for "red bonnet" literally; it's a reference to the red liberty cap, or Phrygian cap, worn by Revolutionaries during the time of the French Revolution.

of incoherent eyes, the path to the heart of a country? At the time, when France had a king, the king represented it in all that was noble and elevated in thought and action, a solid head and valiant heart. "Long Live the King!" logically followed from "The King is Dead!" because the king represented the intelligent and ambitious nation and its public weal; by consequence, to love the king, that meant to love France, and vice versa. Also, what a love the French had for their king, and what patriotism, at that time! But ever since then, when one cried "Long Live the Nation!" it was one's own particular and private weal that one acclaimed, one's private vengeance and particular advancement, it was one's passion and vice that everyone exalted the triumph of; and when, later, to the sound of Santerre's rolling drums and under the flash of Sanson's machine, one can say "The King is Dead," it would have been necessary to add "and France too," if the guillotine had been able to kill both the Monarchy and monarch at the same time.

France has always been quite ill since then, since the cutting off of its head!

The seven cardinal sins, until then checked by laws of the interior forum of conscience where the confessor went to find them and combat them, were pounced on from every side and set up in each and every possible and impossible public function, because improbable employments were edified through satanic foresight, infinitely multiplied in suborder by every capriciousness of revolt and the pullulating lustfulness of ignorance let loose since then. At the same time, ancient despotism, paralyzed since the first Christian kings by episcopal influence and since the time of creation, stone by stone, under the Catholic rule of that marvelous paternity called the French Monarchy, quickly took a breather; and, assuming a new formula, it exceeded at first go, – and how! – the atrocity of the most sinister Caesars, the insolence of the most absurd satraps, and everything offensive that the most unhinged negro chiefs had until then dreamt up for human dignity in their delirious bestiality.

An excess of evil will engender a worse evil. The necessities of a defense to the extreme against an indignant and alarmed Europe gave birth to a militarism of unheard-of intensity on our borders: among a hundred mediocrities and a thousand incapacities in chief, an immense genius logically emerged, the general and administrator of the army. That man[5] amassed anew the power that had "fallen" – in his words, – "into the mud," but, unfortunately raised in Jacobinism, he abused it to the point of usurpation, after having spilt all by himself, a second time, royal blood, as if to burn his ships and hurl himself like a desperate man onto the throne, which was still warm after the massacre in the place Louis XV[6] and the Vincennes ditches.

Ah! he, the new king, who pushed contempt of French Republicans to the point of ridiculing them by his taking the title of Emperor, he was not a father,

[5]That man: Napoleon Bonaparte.

[6]Place Louis XV: later known as the Place de la Concorde (and temporarily known as the Place de la Revolution), it was where King Louis XVI was beheaded in 1793.

but an executioner, who made war like a madman, like a hateful upstart, like a cold dictator by chance, almost a foreigner and completely hostile to the country, which he launched into campaigns of personal ambition. To crown it all with misfortune and chastisement, the conqueror wanted to legislate, and, having naught else in his powerful but culpable head save the Revolution and its principles, he organized chaos and regulated anarchy. Unjust war without, immoral cutbacks within, – and when the hour of his fall sounded, that heart of bronze could make joyous echo, for he left behind him a dismembered country, a stupefied people, – and an entire generation adoring him, soldiers of the old guard, poets, and "liberals"!

The soldiers of the old guard, – good fellows and brave sorts, in sum – passed on, and we have seen the last survivors of them, in worn-out uniforms beneath nervous plumes, come forward with trembling step, to bump up against, at moments of imperial anniversaries, the immortal flower of memory at the solitary railings of the Column. Poets and liberals, them, they made a lasting noise and left behind wee ones. The Napoleonic legend, through familial sympathy whose logic is obscured in our imbecilic times, but which remains in tact in every sane eye, protected the revolutionary "tradition" and soon formed a body with it for the attack and overthrow of that poor Restoration, "which had not restored anything," any more than "learnt anything" from the catastrophes, but rather "forgot everything" of the instructive past. That Restoration! Maladroitly skeptical and surly without vigor, under Louis XVIII, it gropes then, Gallican and incorrect, parliamentarily speaking, under

Charles the Well-Intentioned; it had to perish under
the granted Charter, second manifestation of the Constitution wrested from '91, which, having emasculat-
ed power and making only pitiable concessions, left it
without power at a moment when salutary measures
were finally taken. The work of the Constituent Assembly and Bonaparte remained intact, and Louis-
Philippe, followed by the Revolution of 1848,
Napoleon III, Thiers, and May 16, having respected it
no less scrupulously than Louis XVI's brothers, it had
given birth to those bitter fruits that we see, even under pain of having to eat them to the very last seed,
conservatives that we are!

Alas! everything appears finished, quite finished, for France today! Those so very eloquent de-
feats of 1870-71 seem to have fallen on deaf ears, and
yet it is from then that we date the recrudescence of
evil events, and worse to come, which will be a sign
of our epoch for posterity's horror. Impiety makes
frightening progress together with the Republican
idea, such as the most lost men of first revolution had
understood it; and demagogy has never, for a com-
pressed instant, ferociously and badly, with whatever
energy the bourgeoisie, personified by that deplorable
Thiers, had remaining – that base demagogy has never been on the eve of such a victory. The egoism of
the sensualists now in power, in all the irresponsibili-
ty of a Mayoralty of the palace which is dishonorable
to the first citizen in terms of authority; duplicity
from one day to the next; prevarication of moderation
and effrontery of contradiction (otherwise completely
arbitrary and despotic), which go by the impertinent
name of *opportunism;* cowardly violence; brutal hesi-

tation; all that poor rubbish of Machiavellianism, while succeeding to ruin the last bases of a society that is three-quarters precipitated, while enervating, stupefying, and stunning an electoral body that is made up of all the inferior elements, masks for the mass of dupes, and the worn-out and infatuated people; the imminent supreme abyss; it puts memory to sleep, kills forethought, ruins finally, corrupts, pollutes all faculty, all spirit of conduct, and all vestige of ancient virtue!

No more respect, no more family, shameless pleasure, – what am I saying, the height of debauchery, – zero patriotism, no more conviction, not even bad conviction, no more of the impious heroism of the barricade, with the exception of some déclassés: the "reveler" student; the "thuggish" laborer; the lax ballot box replacing, because of the rioting, the villainous gun, but Frank at least; money for every argument, for every objection, for every victory; idleness and expediency taking their bread from old labor, – and God blasphemed daily, defied, crucified in his church, slapped in his Christ, expropriated, chased, renounced, provoked! What a tribune and what a press! What youth and what women, – and what a country!

But, as it still exists, this horrible France that they have made for us, this difficult France, almost impossible to love, even though one does love it because it still exists, even with its leaders who are not a head,[7]

---

[7]Leaders who are not a head: there is a pun here that is lost in translation: "leaders" in French is "chef" which means head.

even with its rotten members and spoilt blood, even in this pestilential atmosphere, which its evil makes for it, as it still has the body of a nation, as its name subsists and as its tongue is still the first in Europe, it is because, thank God, it *has a heart*, it is because that heart beats still, it is because while it beats, there will be a France that can become the beloved nation of nations again and the soldier of God who made him promises that are almost as solemn as to his Church. From there, it is a matter of getting to that heart other than by memory or imagination; for what the French need, who are jealous of the initial honor and the ever-permitted hope, is the courage to penetrate all hateful and cruel obstacles to the pure and strong source whence issues that gorgeous blood, red and blue, noble, and of the people, whose history was so lovely, which beat at the temples of men of genius as at the feet of charity, as at the flank of the martyr, and which flowed over all the just battlefields and everywhere that God wanted to be glorified by a precious death.

A pious pilgrimage to that sacred fountain, far from the "impure blood" of contemporaries, will revitalize us with hope, and it is with all our French and Christian soul that we will accomplish it. Would that it pleased the reader not to grow discouraged by the numerous pangs and torments along the way. Grievous scenes, sometimes loathsome, often sadly ridiculous, will pass before his eyes. Not a few severe or bitter words will escape us. But everywhere we can, at the expense of the minutest efforts, discover the precious primitive stream, despite all obstructions, under whatever fetid affluence or some other muddy congelation, whatsoever, we will salute the cherished wave, wetting our lips again with its water of glory and faith; and with a more virile step we will take up the pious journey again, assured in God who saves nations as well as men, always French, and French in spite of ourselves, worthy of the ancient name, and proud to hope in so noble a cause!

Chapter 2: Retrospective Glance

But before entering onto the Via Dolorosa,[8] it is important to interrogate the past a little and to borrow the lamp of history in order to shine its light on the wicked *tenebræ* of both politics and present mores. Several words will resume the immediate causes of the Revolution, and from there the contemporary disorder, which is the object of this work.

It is evident that Jansenism, triumphant actually in 1764 after having troubled the church of France for a century with its subtle and not-so-subtle quarrels and dictated in an indirect fashion, but positively, the sad propositions of 1682, held sway, since the time of the Jesuits' expulsion from education, from the pulpit, and from ecclesiastical ministry, under the name of *Gallicanism*, through a hypocrisy and an effrontery even, – and that, in such a way that, in campaigns of the faith, scared off by absurd austerities, deprived almost entirely of the first and most persuasive of the sacraments, in virtue of lamentable scruples, it had gotten to the point of no longer consoling the resignation of the poor. In the cities, the bourgeoisie and artisans, tired of drab and cold sermons where the evangelical flame no longer burned, undecided between

---

[8]Via Dolorosa: Latin for the "Way of Suffering" literally, or the "Way of the Cross" figuratively. It is also the name of a poem by Verlaine in *Cellulely (Cellulairement)*.

the king who said *no* and the parliament that said *yes*
– (the two of them otherwise deciding on dogmatic
matter with an entirely Anglican aplomb) – abandoned the church and flocked to the burgeoning journals, pamphlets, Dutch publications, and to the Encyclopedia, to draw from, for lack of a Pharisaical
Christianity that congealed esoterically in a hard liter-
ality, every sort of doctrine and a completely random
rule of conduct, as the lamp lay under the bush and
the salt of the earth was growing fainter with each
passing day, *cum privilegio*. The convents themselves
let themselves be invaded by a "*not* infrequent com-
munion," and naturally saw vocations abandoned to
reason, in other words to human infirmity, languishing and dying a *natural* death, – that's really the
word, – the supernatural aliment no longer being able
to restrengthen them and give them courage in the
failing hours that everyone, saints included, have
known at the end of their earthly life. The bad example falling from so high could only be rapidly contagious. Curacies and chaplaincies, occupied by priests
imbued for the most part with those maxims, almost
never did apostolic works anymore; and the Gré-
goires[9] and the Siéyès[10] were not the worst among

---

[9]Grégoire: Henri Grégoire (AD 1750-1831) a French abbot or
prelate. He apparently opposed the coup d'état of 18 Brumaire
(Nov 9, 1799). He was a defender of the nationalized French
Church during the Revolution and of the Constitutional Church,
which was abolished by the Concordat of 1801.

[10]Siéyès: Emmanuel Joseph Siéyès (or *l'abbé Siéyès*) (AD 1748-
1836), a Roman Catholic clergyman, politician and essayist. He
was also one of the Directors during the French Consulate.
Famous among other things for having been, together with
Talleyrand, responsible for the coup d'état on 18 Brumaire (Nov
9, 1799) which overthrew the Directory and effectively both

those strange pastors of souls. The colleges, almost all of which were in the hands of the degenerate Oratorians,[11] teemed with unbelieving professors; the Daunous and so many others had in truth so many other problems than simply that of teaching virtue and science to an already rebellious youth, as those poor but so very despised Jesuits had done. Themselves attacked hour after hour by skepticism, without any other defense against the mounting incredulity than an impossible refuge in an afflicted calvary, bristling with thorns, where the Jansenists of the first hour had crucified a "Christ" with obstinate eyes turned towards the irritated Father, with arms raised to heaven from which he seemed to regret having descended; those Oratorians, those city and country priests whose theological studies were so distorted, raised in a forced respect for the State, almost to the exclusion of the obedience owed to Peter's See, and naturally biased as to which side they must fall on; and utopias were in ferment in those failed educations; ideas of literal equality, of speculative freedom, overran their teachings and succeeded in forming the soul of a Robespierre, a Camille, while monstruous Constitutions were worked out in those troubled minds over the ruins of poorly-understood, unrecognized Scriptures, rejected in the final analysis and weary of war! – O Arnauld, Nicole,[12] and Pascal, madman of genius and vicious man, who passes for a saint, angel and beast, you who tired of the charity of doubting your

ended the Revolution and inaugurated Napoleon Bonaparte's rise to power.

[11]Oratorians: the Congregation of the Oratory of Saint Philip Neri, created in 1575.

definitive damnation or salvation because of a candid
bad faith and ingenuous fanaticism; you, daughters of
Port-Royal, angels of purity, if not demons of pride,
even you, the least convulsionists of good faith, –
what shame, what penance, and what a return to Peter
and his faithful, if you could only have seen in that
work, your last and almost unconscious disciples:
Lebon and Gobel! Not to mention your names and
your works (never read, and for good reason!), always
invoked and thrown into the face of cordial and effec-
tive Faith, which those great Jesuits still represent,
more glorious than ever, by all that the rottenness of
the times engenders in the enemies of Christ and his
Church!

It is clear that a Catholicism thus hardened, shrunken,
could not take any action against mores any more
than against ideas. The detestable Regency and the
sad example of a king left to the worst courtiers were
responsible for the corruption that spilled over from
court to city, and from city to countryside. The obscene literature of philosophers, the relaxation of convents, the escarpment, so to speak, of essential sacraments that were prisoners of a pitiless sect the last
tenants of which (in Holland) symbolize quite well
the horrible error, by characteristic practices, such as,
during mass, the priests raising the host and the chal-
ice with their right hand only, their left hand repre-
senting those for whom Christ is not dead, – by whom

---

[12]Arnauld, Nicole: Antoine Arnauld (AD 1612-1694) and Pierre
Nicole (AD 1625-1695), Jansenist co-authors of *La Logique de
Port-Royal.*

predestination and grace are interpreted completely
askew, – respect for the Pope and for the king tread
on by parliamentarians confederated with theologians
of the thing; the example of imprudence haughtily
given by these latter as by the former while pretend-
ing to remain in the Church that anathematized them
and in the kingdom that condemned them by its chief;
the entirely natural doubt whereby such attitudes consecrated by incontestable talent and *respectability* of
rebellious principals could not fail to make the minds
of the common people waver; the subsequent hesita-
tion to fulfill the clearest duties and taking aim at
chimerical rights; such dispositions, fomented in the
midst of the most rapid dissolution of all moral and
social bonds, fatally went on to blossom into what
one has seen, – and I ask you for a moment just what
such an upheaval must produce, if not the arrival of
worse in place of the bad, and bad in place of the
good?

And if we brusquely come back to our definitive times, it is a remark that all competent men, curates, vicars, and missionaries have made, that the re-
gions of France where that sect has most reigned are
the most indifferent to religious matters, by consequence the most lax as far as morals go, and the most
intellectually Republican today, after otherwise having been that diabolical invention that we will speak
about in a moment, according to the *material* interest
of the times, by all parties, according to the traditional
practices of universal suffrage.

An important observation must still be made
in this chapter before we can in all surety approach

things of the present: the ill-fated movement of the
16th century, under its two forms, the Renaissance – (a
despicable usage has consecrated that deceptive de-
nomination; it should be called the *Reaction* instead)
– and the Reformation, (yet another odious linguistic
untruth) – has found, from the time of its origin, an
unrelenting, implacable adversary in the Society of
Jesus, founded on militant humility and respect in direct opposition and similar to a strategy, with a spirit
of insubordination and pride that that double evolution toward evil implicated. The admirable militia of
Saint Ignatius triumphed, in the measure desired by
God, over the bicephalous monster, in Europe and
particularly in France, over the course of several tragic peripeteia, as everyone knows, and in spite of
calumnies and such heated prejudices that still mill
about and bite in our days. By the grace of predica-
tions, missions, their precious instruction, the Jesuits
made the French 17th century one of complete faith,
dignity, knowledge, authority, and in which art and
literature reacted so entirely against the voluptuous
paganism of the preceding epoch. I say nothing about
their splendid works of faith and legislation throughout all the universe, but limit myself to my own country which they gave so high a place to, as soon as they
were free.

But Satan was watching, and, sensing that
Protestantism was down for the count in France, took
his work back in hand and, so as better to succeed, re-
sorted to his old ruse, disguising himself as an angel of
light once again: whence primitive Jansenism, its aus-
terity, its protestations, alas as eloquent and brilliant as
it was hypocritical and perfidious, by the organ of a

writer of genius against intelligent indulgence and the entirely evangelical mansuetude of Jesuit casuists, whence we have, in a nation that is above all generous and quick to chime in with beautiful words, the popularity of those ferocious doctrines that suppressed all gentleness and breadth in the examination of cases of conscience, in the name of an impracticable, distressing morality, but speaking at a much higher level than it and of it alone, as if it were the only Christian morality and true perfection. Twenty times since, probative refutations by decree and especially in action broke out, which left not a vestige of detestable error subsisting; the Holy See struck down the tortuous heresy in no uncertain terms. It made no difference. The blow to the Jesuits and to orthodox Catholicism had succeeded and was made to resound until our own days. Henceforth, without a sure guide, the faith of the feeble, that is to say, of the multitude, took fright and turned from scruple to indifference, and from there to all the mistakes that afflict us [today].

Chapter 3: Of Universal Suffrage and the Concordat of 1801

It goes without saying that the social abasement procured by events in the latter part of the eighteen century should culminate in a system that is the last word on individual degradation.

The year of stupidity of 1848 witnessed the blossoming of that most insane thing of all the insanities of the epoch. A resounding orator, without a trace of politics in his head, became the champion of Universal Suffrage, and the riotous government bowed its head in the naïve enthusiasm raised by the proposition, considered popular by those off-the-rails bourgeois.[13] What remained of common sense, not yet evaporated, made the henceforth "active" masses vote for an assembly that was absolutely hostile to the experiment, and the following year saw a voting system based on suffrage censitaire, – for the most part detestable as well, although a little less so – which was restored by the very same people whom the new electoral colleges had appointed.

It would be as superfluous as fastidious to trace out the developments that everyone knows, the comedy of Universal Suffrage since its reestablish-

---

[13] A resounding orator...: possibly Louis Blanc (AD 1811-1882) a journalist, French historian, and deputy of the French Third Republic, who championed universal suffrage.

ment in 1851.

That would be, also, to catch sempiternal human stupidity in the act once again, cubed this time and acting on that deplorable stage, the Fatherland! We prefer to remove from contemplation of such a prodigy of sloppiness all the melancholic moralities that it implies.

To begin with, does it not strike you that those two words *Universal Suffrage*, compared with the actual thing, impudently lie? – In effect, the mass of voters being a compound of ignorance and strict egoism, how not to see that its votes will always be tainted, if they had rallied around a single name by an insolent preoccupation of pure self-interest, influenced by such and such artificial agent, corruption, or propaganda. The *esprit de corps*, without which society is not possible, such that the mere mention of that truth brings a smile to the lips of the most scatterbrained individuals, the *esprit de corps*, a union deficient in electoral operations, what sort of government is to be hoped for by a parliament thus nominated? And it is in vain to object that such parties, as events have made them, exist only by the grace of that union and can supplement that incontestable need for national cohesion with the superiority even that they act by free will and in fruitful competition. The response is too facile, and no one can deny that our political parties are, without exception, miserable coalitions merely of interested individuals, – while naturally disregarding the more-or-less disinterested individualities who comprise them (and here also we lapse again into a fatal dissipation), – given that, with the ballot in question, nothing moves without these sordid masses, our absolute masters, and that it is only by appealing to individual interests that one can hope to have them on one's side. If to these considerations you add, for the record, that the pulverization of our free provinces into subservient departments has merely anticipated the evil and generalized the spirit of divisiveness, and non-government, hatched in 1789, – if you compare the Upper and Lower Houses and the Presidencies of limited suffrage (quite mediocre, however, in its last period especially) to those of Universal Suffrage over the last fifteen years, since its emancipation more or less, you will shudder to imagine the ruins that it leads us to, launched as it is today along its logical tendency and directed by the men you know. The ancient constitution of France, the only serious one, the only practical one, the only one that would have lasted and had a chance of resurrection, even though and *because* it was not written down,[14] took good care not to fail, – formed as it was over the centuries and amended by the slow evolutions of a legitimate authority, – to be conformant with the one principle of every government destined to last. It rested on that *esprit de corps* which the immense Joseph de Maistre has given a magnificent definition of, with respect precisely to those same Jesuits we mentioned earlier and who will have a considerable role to play in the aftermath of that work: "the annihilation of particular wills in order to establish a general will and that common reason which is the generative and conservative principle of every institution whatsoever, great or

---

[14]The ancient constitution...: in reference presumably to certain rules of Salic Law, scil., inheritance and agnatic succession.

small." The division of the nation into three Orders, invested, each for its own part, with these three primordial rights: vote and conservation of the *laws of the realm* (rule of succession to the crown in the absence of a male heir, election of a king in the case of extinction of the dynasty); establishment of taxes; necessary consent for the validation of any perpetual alienation of the domain or any partial dismemberment of the realm, – they gave every guarantee of security and dignity to the country and had this other advantage of exonerating the *executive* – to employ that word which Republican desire has deemed belittling to supreme authority and which is only for the bit of power that the system leaves in the hands of its "delegates" for the execution of its laws, with all the responsibility of a purely collective order, leaving it free and powerful for everything else that needs to be done. What is more, let us observe and keep in mind that each of the three Orders, restricted to the examination of and demand for its needs, with every jealousy or ambition that lies outside that venerated circle being unknown to those assemblies, which are devoted since then to a single objective: the advancement and honor of the Body for the good of the Public Thing – could only do useful and noble work within its concerns. Competitions and rivalries among them, no example of it until 1789; Catholicism imposed its light yoke on those consecrated and baptized foreheads, and justice prevailed among the several differences of opinion that were inseparable from every human debate. The King's word was respectfully heard; that of his representatives, jurists, and senechals was discussed in complete national independence, as well as in every Christian courtesy; they dominated the discussion and, when necessary, brought minds back to the common goals for assembly: everyone's interest and the country's glory. Never have more august assizes decided broader matters, – thanks to the wise economy of the established rule (today one would say regulation), not by such and such men, such and such amendment, entrusted for their protection to any old removable questor, but over the course of the ages, according to opportunities or general dangers arising, and placed under faith of oath and guardianship of Tradition, – without producing conflicts of egoism and vanity that make the deliberations, one might say, of all our modern parliaments so petty, so sterile, and often so hateful, the which parliaments are based merely on a suffrage that is like shifting sand, dependent on the chance occurrence of tumultuous and crazy constitutions, like the wind.

That some abuses had sometimes broken out in those majestic Cortès,[15] – attempts at usurpation, in complicity with the street or with foreigners disguised as pretenders, as for example in the reign of Charles the Wise, – one would need to have a poor understanding of humanity to be overly surprised by it; but also the other side of the Constitution acted as a counterweight, and royal authority, invested with no less a secular respect than with powerful privileges indispensable to its immense responsibility and strong in the conscience of its sublime mandate, always managed to procure again the salvatory balance. In 1789, the Third Estate broke the old order. The two other

---

[15]Cortès: legislative assemblies (particularly in Spain and Portugal).

Orders, enervated by Jansenism and corrupted by philosophism, lacked the vigor to react; moreover, royalty, three-quarters of which had suicided because of the blind goodness and capricious feebleness of a poorly advised prince, had to disappear so that one might consider the horror of the chasm that it filled and its providential place in our country. Everything crumbled.[16]

The Edifice, destroyed for the fault of the Third Estate, took some time before foundering entirely, and today we can see the last catastrophes sapping it, that unfortunate Third Estate, making it go and join the Nobility and the Clergy at the bottom of the revolutionary pit, admirable punishment for the first word it spoke when it departed for war: "the Third must be everything!" Read the red journals today, or simply the Tricolor ones, and recall the early successes they had in March 1871. Is it not possible to predict that the bourgeoisie will soon be nothing? – Yes, by the grace of the last Order's anti-patriotic infatuation, at an epoch when the Estates General should have saved everything, by inaugurating patient reforms through a vigorous and offensive resistance to the mounting revolution, we have arrived, in less than one hundred years, at the shame of being a bleating rabble led to the slaughterhouse by a lie!

---

[16]Original foonote: Note by the author: The *esprit de corps* was not contained entirely in the Estates General, but had deep roots throughout the country: jurandes, corporations, assemblies of peace, communes, formed, in some sort, the basis of that great national representation, that "fourth Estate," the people, robust caryatid of the State properly speaking. That strong foundation of ancient France will be discussed at the proper time. This note is only *for order's sake*.

From the results, in some sort physical, of that immense change in our constitutional life, – results that
we have just tried to summarize in a few lines, – if we
pass over to the results that I would call chimerical, to
the new morality, to the daily incidents in private life,
it would not be one volume, but rather a library of details and examples that would need be written. Moreover, most of the chapters that follow are merely an
attempt to abridge a similar work, and, just as was
promised earlier, we will never lose sight of it, not the
least encouraging symptom, nor the harmful influence, latent or disclosed, of the demoralizing suffrage
in question. For the moment, it will be enough for us
to point out the enormous humiliation of the French
people since they forged the chains of 1789 and
passed through the hands of each of the masters who
wanted to make themselves feared or served. One of
the characteristics of that humiliation is the all new
patience with which this people accepts and suffers
the heaviest burdens ever imposed on them by their
elected officials. All possible taxes on the least likely
taxable stuff, a military service that is increasingly
crushing and repugnant to them, the administration
growing heavier and more unrestrained every year, all
this passes over us French people like a sheepdog
through a flock [of sheep]. They get in line and align
with a submission that they refuse to the Good Pastor
himself. And the reason for this was explained to me
recently by a future elector, a young man otherwise
brimming with commonsense, heart, and judgment
for his age, and who will certainly go back over his
opinion of today which I give to you in all the green-

ness of his twentieth French year: "What do you want? At least these people, if they tyrannize me, I WILL DENOUNCE THEM!" Madness shared by the the majority of people, even the elderly. (What strange elderly we have today and those of tomorrow!) Ah! in the Year II of execrable memory, the man of the people, quite lost clearly, quite mad, participated at least in the tyranny and counted on his own violence: he pillaged, he worked in the fields stolen by him the day before, and when he had to defend that ill-gotten property, he gave his blood to the armies, or took the blood of legitimate possessors or heirs, either by force, hatchet in hand, or by a goodly public denunciation to his section. Sometimes also the feeling of righteousness carried him along in heroic insurrections. He claimed ancient liberties and mixed the old monarchic faith with the federalist tendencies of the Center and the Midi. In Brittany, in the Vendée, religious persecution and military requisition roused the entire population and what followed was a gigantic war, without parallel in the annals of any nation. Those noble sons of the plow relied on their solid simplicity and delved deeply into the rectitude of their conscience for the energy of twenty armies in order to resist the all-powerful evil, to keep it at bay and hold it in check for many years, and they vouchsafed the honor of faithfulness and French commonsense in the eyes of the world and that of the future! They had every reason just as they had every courage, those headstrong Vendéens, those obstinate Chouans. That which they defended so fiercely with their Faith and their King, it was the independence of their homes and their labor, which Faith and King had guaranteed them for centuries; it was the equitable tax, the tithe, and the gabelle, until then gladly ceded in their gratitude, and which were destined to be replaced by taxes a hundred times more vexing, besides which deplorably introduced and odiously collected; it was the spirit of their ancestors, piously accepted and obeyed; it was the life and future, the soul and heart, of their children that the terrorist laws menaced, the work of the rebel assassins of Paris! By a splendid intuition of their ardent Catholicism, they placed on their ensigns and wore on their clothes the image of the Sacred Heart of Jesus,[17] as if to attest to their being indeed the France of the Church, abounding in the graces of heaven and consumed by an immense gratitude, the soldiers of the God of love and purity in battle against the criminal France of the Encyclopedia and the filthiest faubourgs of a new Gomorrah, themselves the proud peasants tanned in a paternal sun, contemplators and intimates of the great dawns and great waves, deaf like their rocks to the Parisian dementia, and like them the guardians and witnesses of a solid earth, devouring, virgin, the last refuge, the terrible citadel of Tradition!

But the people of today! They accept all prejudice coming at them from those whom they carried on their shield for one or two years; they calmly watch as injustice is inflicted on their neighbor, – for envy con-

---

[17]Original footnote: Note by the author: It is only in the last years that one has learnt that the Blessed Marguerite-Marie has received revelations concerning France and the Royal House. For the story of these latest revelations and their connection with the war in the Vendée, as well as more recent and no less beautiful manifestations, read the fine work by M. Abbot Bougaud on the Origins of the devotion for the Heart of Jesus.

sumes his heart, – and if that injustice catches them in passing, no less calmly will they hold their tongue, and smile sallowly, all the while swearing that they will vote *better* "the next time" and, when the next time comes around, things will go from bad to worse. We have seen this happen twenty times over, and we will see it happen a hundred times, if God will not take pity on us until the very end. Every dignity, every act of civil courage, every public exertion, even a little generous, died at the precise moment that Universal Suffrage came into practice. Do not speak to me about the June of 1848, or about the Commune of 1871: uprisings fabricated in their entirety and for a long time by the Freemasons and their recent branch, the International, by dint of newspapers, money, and a recruitment in every country, at times famine and an extraordinary craziness in narrow-minded heads overheated by intoxicated misery; zero spontaneity in those two *issues* of socialist forces: slogan and compulsion! – No, for the moment, and for some time now, the platitude contains us, both cities and countrysides, bourgeois and others! – The loathsome platitude, and stupider than loathsome, because frighteningly loathsome! A fierce cowardice giving credit to a tyranny at once deceitful and cynical, the very meaning of the words lacking for those who speak, just as for those who listen, in that government of prattlers, so much so that *liberty*, in their slang, means *prerogative to do anything*, and for others the *right to inflict harm*; every principle whatsoever, moral or political, absolutely absent in their minds and hearts, pure and simple animality, and bestiality crouching behind it, ready to pounce, – so that look at us now, the French of 1881, after ninety years of democracy and thirty-t-wo years of direct Universal Suffrage!

There could have been a remedy, there was only one remedy, a remedy that, well applied, could have fixed everything, could have put everything back into its place even, and, you have guessed it, it is religion, it is its general policy. Now, the religious policies in France, the nation, are the Concordat of 1801 – that of 1817 being for all intents and purposes dead, and when one examines it in itself, the Concordat of 1801 presents the minimum guarantee for the Church, and there is nothing surprising in that, given that the con-tracting party who represented the French State, all powerful at that time, was strong enough to abuse the natural willingness of the Holy See to go out of its way for an immediate reestablishment of Catholicism in France, at any price. (But Rome always does well at what it does, and the evil that could have been in-troduced by papal concessions in that circumstance is the act of the politicians of that country.) Whatever the case might be, that Concordat, considered as an instrument of religious propaganda, is a most defec-tive piece of work, better than nothing, yes, but hardly much more than that, we have to admit.

Besides, the results are in. In Bonaparte's mind, the Church had to be auxiliary to the Adminis-tration, nothing more; for it to depend on the Pope, the nation would need to remain Catholic, and that detestable man of genius was too clever not to appre-ciate all that the Catholic Church, the Catholic Church alone, could do for moral and even material

order in France, – but at least the nation would depend on it as little as possible, and for that, among a
thousand other Gallican precautions, the wily Corsi-
can fox was careful to omit from that new organization the holy militia, religious congregations, and
front and rear guards of the secular clergy; and we
have seen where that omission can lead in the hands
of wicked men. The episcopacy saw itself nearly as-
similated into the bureaucracy and subject to a thousand small-minded constraints. The "cult" – "salar-
ied" meagerly moreover, – together with heresy and
deicide, was in the master's mind no more than a
piece of that vast empire which he had turned into one
of the most powerful war engines, and if that master
saw himself forced to admit the Pope like a drive
shaft and the *cardinals* of the Sacred College like
hinges, make no mistake about it, he intended to have
control over them, like an engine driver, and to make
the Church move within the State, no more no less!
The new clergy, composed of poor, unexperienced,
heterogenous elements, who had to assume this task
before God: the restoration of the French Church and
the education of a half-savage people, – poorly remu-
nerated, who were not encouraged but harassed, on
the contrary, by suspicions from above and by unpop-
ularity from below, could only be admirable in the
fulfillment of its duty and did not fail, but, lacking serious means (insufficient recruitment, pecuniary difficulties for the needs of the apostolate, so many other
causes of weakness!), the progress it made was too
slow in the minds of the people, and the family often
succeeded in undermining its work insofar as children
were concerned, for example, the heathen family and

worse, for six mortal years of complete forgetfulness of religion and the accumulation of fierce biases. To summarize all the vice of the system in one single example, – what is one hour of catechism a week compared to paternal examples in three quarters of the cases, and maternal ignorance, even then when the mother has some religion and some concern for [her children's] education? Also, see what indifference exists in the people of the countryside and what hostility in those of the city as far as Catholic things are concerned. We will not insist here on that lamentable outcome of the sad Concordat of 1801. A good part of this book will treat of it.

Besides, our prolegomena have come to an end, and we proceed to the heart of the matter, which lies open to our investigation henceforth and is capricious in appearance, even though we claim to apply a strict method to it; precisely for this reason, we thought it was our duty to begin by making observations that will command all those that follow.

Chapter 4: About Sundays in France[18]

O Work! merciful chastisement of sin, originally designed by the Creator for the enjoyment of the leisure of innocence, then made severe by man's own fault, who carried it with him, the last and only memory of earthly Paradise, a consolation as well as a duty, and a distraction as much as a holy debt, the punished man's reason for existing, his dignity also, a reminder of his first privilege, his solvency for all the advances of Grace and Mercy, – who, better than a Catholic, would understand you, would honor you? Who would practice you better, more gaily, more meritoriously, with more order, intelligence, and honorable profit? I attest to an arable Europe, a literary antiquity restored to our admiration, and the monks of the early Christian period of our Occident. I attest to the architectural immensity of the great centuries of faith, their theological and political depth, their social work, their chemical research, their trials, their successes in astronomy, – and the ardent navigation, exclusively Christian, completely propagandistic, of the epochs that followed immediately afterwards. I attest to the modern Church and its indefatigable laborers, from the Jesuits, in all things excellent workers at all hours,

---

[18]Sundays in France: see also Léon Bloy's *She Who Weeps*, wherein he discusses that the two greatest concerns of La Salette for France and the entire world, at the time of the Holy Virgin Mary's Apparition, were blasphemy and the inobservance of the Sabbath. Bloy makes reference to this posthumous work by Verlaine, and to this chapter in particular.

to the creators, founders, and administrators of universities, colleges, seminaries, primary schools, workshops, orphanages, and Catholic circles, not to mention so many other institutions of pure activity that prosper and grow on the just ruins of an enraged persecutive competition, patient because eternal, eternal because divine! I see work honored and practiced among us Christians and above all among us French, – honored and practiced under all ancient and modern forms, and my Christian heart cannot help but beat with pride and joy at the sight of Christian work, all Christian work, that is to say the only true work, and how I love, o how ardorously! and venerate *real* laborers, while my charity grows interested in all fairness for others, who have gone astray but are valiant all the same, pities them, these workers, and desires with all its heart their glorious return, their ever blessed reconciliation.

Alas! being French, I know them, those workers outside the fold, whom a terrible habit of indifference, – a crime of education, – goads on to the forbidden work; I know them, living near them, being nearly one of them, I respect them for their courage throughout the week, and I pity their ignorance as to the meaning of Sunday, murderous ignorance that makes that day, in France, a hideous phenomenon, a lugubrious curiosity for the foreigner – whoever he might be! – traveling here.

There was a law against working on Sunday, a law otherwise abrogated in recent past by the people one knows, but because of that national ignorance it finds itself scandalously violated by a people ordinari-

ly so supple, but who subject themselves to every
servitude. The only concern left in the French heart,
to enrich itself, together with a lack of confidence in
an almost unknown God, had erased from our life that
vivifying, only vivifying thing, the respect for Sunday. – "The clouds are gathering. To the fields!
Woman, prepare the soup for noon sharp. We will set
out after the horses have eaten." – "A good wedding
Monday. It's Lacoterie who treats. No work on Sunday."

And that happens weekly in serenity, in complete security, in the village henceforth as in the city.

The wife sometimes goes to Low Mass, and
sometimes she objects. But the husband, if on an
empty stomach, sniggers and worse; if the morning
drop was strong, he revolts, and yells out about the
"curates." – "All that will change! Your daughter will
know more than you do, now that they are getting rid
of religious devotion at school. And long live the Republic!"

The child hears these expressions, the majority of the time punctuated by blasphemies, observes
these inobservances. In some families of this same
sort, when one sends the child to mass, because the
father does not go and because the father does not fail
to proclaim at every opportunity his superiority of intelligence and instruction (o save us!), moreover because the most anti-Christian journals lie everywhere
about the house and are read, commented on, exalted
in the evenings except when the man comes home too
drunk or too tired from working his parcel of ill-gotten land or from some other despotic, vile, and rude

industry, the revenge of so-called old privileges mur-
dered by the grandparents, – the child in whom the
seeds of insurrection are planted by that horrible education, well in advance of adulthood, becomes corrupted terribly early on, uses his reason wrongly, and
turns out logically worse than his sad forebears. And
so on and so forth since 1789. Are you surprised now!

For the observation of Sunday is *entirely* from
the first revelation: God's 1st commandment that "you
shall worship." From which all civilization (in the
true sense) flows.

Oh! after six days of work accepted, adorned,
embellished, nourished by those cries of love and
hope, ejaculative orisons, so highly touted, how sweet
it is to rest one's tired limbs in God, one's weary
head, and to be all love, all gratefulness for the immense Paternity, the infinite Kindness! To be one
with the family, that family that nothing can destroy,
neither the oft-accused sin, absolved and rarified from
day to day, nor persecution from without, taken in
pity and resolved in prayers for the persecutors, nor
death which will be a reunion in joy without end! To
be there, father, mother, children, quietly happy in the
lush garden, around a large fire if one is wealthy,
filled with gratitude for one's repose, at ease for the
grace of one's neighbor if one is poor, – a Christian
society I suppose. Isn't that right, as one says, and as
one says about Christian marriage, an earthly Paradise
regained, and a celestial Paradise enjoyed one day a
week?

And then

"tabernacula tua!"

Hear the church bells ringing with the sounds of the flute and horn, grave and joyous sounds, and harken to their fresh call. What a serene and penetrating joy, expansive too, to be present at these divine offices, at the adorable Sacrifice, at these Vespers unfurling like waves of incense until the incense of the *Magnificat*, and the *Tantum ergo*. Overabundance of benediction for the soul, sanctification and noble delight of the senses to which an entire part of these majestic sessions is directed by the maternal wisdom of the Catholic liturgy.

On exiting the Church, these faces are dignified, their eyes shine more calmly and deeply, their hands are found to be more active in the giving of alms to the good, poor people, all joyous themselves in the blessed atmosphere of Sunday.

England, of all countries, has in particular preserved these august and charming traditions: those Protestants put great pride in it even. Not just great pride, but just pride. Of course, heresy has in part withered that work of salvation; it has brought that exaggeration, that literal indiscretion that kills instead of vivifies the "supererogatory" Catholic things; still, it is just to render homage to the incontestable dignity which public mores and the manifestations of thought, literature, art, Parliamentary debates, the press, gain by that initial and principal observation. The family spirit, still very strong and hierarchical in that country which nevertheless allowed itself to be won over by the anarchistic doctrines of the continent, is due, to be sure, as much to the observance of

Sunday at home and at Temple as to the very judi-
cious preservation of the father's freedom to be-
queath. Their material prosperity, so to speak, which
does not stop crowning the enterprises and operations
of that empire, derives quite clearly from the entirely
special benediction that is attached to the good cus-
tom that we refer to, and if Catholic nations, *without
exception*, – take good note of it, – are inferior in everything, anarchic and unfortunate in nearly all re-
spects, do you not see in it, with the eyes of the faithful, – the eyes alone! – a paternal chastisement from
on high for the profanation of the Holy Day by these
ungrateful and *thick-headed* people, like Israel, their
prophetic symbol, who were unable to hold on to their
gift of God and precipitated themselves headfirst into
ineptitude, filth, and the abominable French Revolution finally. And while these nations, France, alas! out
in front, lose a little of their fathers' faith with each
passing day, with all their former virtues, and roll ver-
tiginously forward to the last *tenebræ* of the dirtiest
atheism, admire how England and America, faithful
guardians of dominical rest, – magnificent recompense! – admire how all those men of good faith in
their churches return to the one Church, and in daily
groups, in incessant crowds.

But France is loved by God all the same. The
intense, intelligent, patriotic and provident compassion of our ancestors gained us splendid indulgences
and the grace stays with us, indefatigable.

She whom one never invokes in vain has, in recent days, multiplied in luminous words her quietly
imperious desire *to be invoked* in diverse parts of our

territory. One of the principal instances of those merciful visits insisted most particularly – and in what a touching and strong way! – on the absolute necessity of the observance of Sunday. The tears and threats of La Salette, the promises of Lourdes and Pontmain, countless mercies and terrifying punitions, new works, pilgrimages more flourishing than ever, noble sufferances and courageous oppositions in response to 1793, serene and probable expectation of a martyrdom, expiations for the faith, – how many proofs, how many hopes, what near certitude of seeing France lift itself up again by those two first commandments finally understood anew, and joyously obeyed! Mary, so often invoked in her sanctuaries which were chosen, it might be said, for that merciful purpose, can do no more than utter, once again, for us and for our children her all powerful *Fiat!*

While waiting, – what a shame for France!

Chapter 5: To My Son

I imagine myself [to have] a son old enough to be a soldier, and, supposing all hypotheses favorable to my reasoning, I imagine my saying to him or writing to him as follows:

"The day of glory" has arrived then, my dear child, the R. F.[19] of 1880 "forms its battalions." It "calls its children" as the "France" of 1848 did. And the "volunteers" respond to its voice, the volunteers appropriated to the enthusiasms that it excites, the volunteers of one year, *in other words* the "men of conditional enlistment" or, as one says to the regiment, "the conditionals" quite simply.

Your age designates you for the army, and your education admits you among those privileged men of the last hour; for there are rumors of a supreme conquest of democracy, of Desire, I say, which governs us (if that is what it means to govern!). It is really a matter, it appears, of shredding, for next year, that testament of commonsense in the tragic organization of our army. The directive causing such combative ardor amongst our masters, to make money, their god, and the god of so many others, their electors, – will no longer save anyone from the fatal standard. "Everybody a soldier!" Desire exclaimed, and the echo in German responds: "nobody a soldier!"[20]

---

[19]R. F.: French Republic.

[20]Original footnote: Note by the author: There is need to insist on that truth, a thousand times evoked since the sad legislation of

But, after all, that does not concern us, and as it is the virtue of this century to be egotistical, let's be egotistical for a little while and pat ourselves on the back by taking advantage, the last ones to do so, of a liberty that will go the way of all others – a liberty moreover well paid for, to those merchants of anarchy!

There you are then, a soldier for one year. One year, what is that compared to four? – Little, almost nothing in truth, for the price of four, – even though that is already too much as time passes, for a father anxious for the soul as much as, if not more so than, the material well-being of his only son. And you have already guessed it, your Christian heart has understood that I cannot let you depart

> *"... O the best part*
> *Of me..."*

without the viaticum of a brief and heartfelt word, a direct counsel, that will accompany you, guide you, and defend you, when the time comes, along the strange paths that you will need to take.

'73, that the Prussian system itself had been born as a result of the precarious situations that Napoleon had reduced the recruitment of the German army to, after Jena, and it was not in short but a stopgap measure, an indirect means to supplement a derisory strength imposed on them by the most ruthless of victors. But the Mediocrity that predominated in '73, while waiting for the rascals we now see, found nothing better than to adapt to our necessities of that period and which – o prodigy of imbecility! left to act in complete freedom, – was the empirical means of patriotism of an entirely different temperament, driven to supreme expedients.

To begin with, let me reassure myself of the idea that
you are a Christian; that security, for which I thank
God every day as the immense recompense of some
efforts of education, is strengthened also by the
knowledge, acquired by my paternal solicitude, of
your character, decidedly serious all the while lov-
able, ingenuous without awkwardness, and delicate
without timidity or dupery. A prompt and fervent de-
cision for action guarantees for me your return to
goodness in the event of disaster. The return to goodness is a rough road that must be traveled at all costs,
through all fatigues and whatever might crop up along
the way.

In an agglomeration of all sorts of men (as
much to say that today in the army the unit predomi-
nates) under a regime like that which absurd Numbers
have made for us, and in the fetid times we traverse
like someone traversing through a grimy fog, the
worst stumbling block would be, for a practicing
Catholic like you even, that thing, French since 1789,
cowardly at all times and particularly culpable today,
– human Respect. I am almost afraid of greatly up-
setting you by evoking the suspicion that you could
stub your toe against that vile pebble and stumble,
and provoke on your lips a filial reply *à la Rodrigue*,
but, my dear child, it is precisely one of the ruses of
that Devil we believe in, we ourselves, then when his
most precious agents disown him while denying him
– (he is not proud, the Devil!) – it is, I say, one of the
best tricks of the Wicked to put such contemptible obstacles in front of his most general adversaries which
they don't pay enough attention to and which they often fall cruelly for. Illustrious examples of human re-

spect ought to make us tremble, and infinite Compassion has doubtless permitted them merely to warn us, solemnly, of the extreme malice inherent in that weakness: if a Peter[21] was able to renounce his master thrice, what must we not fear, weaklings that we are, from our pusillanimity?

Be strong then against human Respect. And note well that in this counsel to you I imply no indiscreet zeal. Do your complete duty as a Christian, without concern for sots or any other bad actors, without propaganda, except that all-powerful one of example.

The method is quite simple for making peace with the sad villains of impiety or the brutes of indifference whom you are unfortunately sure to encounter; it is this: avoid their company, even if brusquely. The amiability, then, that a clear conscience unfailingly adds to the conversation, to the general manners of being and living, in short, to the whole individual, will vanquish every exterior bad will, except perhaps on the rare exceptions in which a firm attitude, but always dignified and polite, would effect prompt justice, to be sure. Moreover, in case of difficulties, God is there, and his Holy Spirit invoked each day in your prayers will always know how to inspire in you the conduct and words that you need to take or employ.

I just spoke about words, and I was speaking earlier about the propaganda of example. They are

---

[21]Peter: in reference to Simon-Peter, but also Pierre, which in French means stone or rock, and which harkens back to the "pebble" mentioned earlier.

precisely, in your present situation, in complete corre-
lation, to the degree almost of being one and the
same. What I mean by that is that in service, even at
that moment of the first deterioration and slackening
of discipline, *action* is inevitably good, insofar as
there could be scandal! A paternal severity sternly
suppresses drunkenness or nocturnal lust; obedience
is the first duty and, if ignored, is severely avenged;
so much so that unless one is a pure scoundrel, or a
stubborn fool, it is much easier to fulfill all the duties
of a soldier than to expiate the least infraction of this
rigid program however disagreeable that might be...
But *conversation*, in the barracks, let's talk about
that! All the criminal hideousness of blasphemy is
bound up there with the most ignominious obscenity.
A Christian ear or simply an honest one bleeds with
each word that is heard – in this, there is no protection, no recourse within the rule. The rule is deaf to
such legitimate subtleties and silent on this article.
The leaders, for the most part, set the example and go
further in tone than their inferiors, and there is, from
the congestion of the major, liquored up on absinthe,
to the rattle of the newly commissioned sublieutenant
from Saint-Cyr,[22] a gamut of swear words and filthy
jokes that the "men" are only all too ready to sing,
them also, given so good an example they have, – and
more cynically still!

This is the "tradition"... since that ignoble
1789. Where is that time when officers addressed
their soldiers as "Gentlemen masters," and politeness
flourished alongside piety in the camps?

---

[22]Saint-Cyr: the special military academy located in Brittany,
founded by Napoleon Bonaparte in 1802.

And where is the Monarchy?

Eh well, as the example, – which is a tad bit useless insofar as concerns the *action* in the barracks, where acting even is a condition *sine qua non* of an existence not-too-unbearable, – whereas the example finds its first opportunity there, with respect to *expression*, that is to say that it offers an admirable occasion for Charity, you, being "well spoken," set the tone for those who address you. Never condescend to speak a single triviality even, nor to laugh about one. As for swearing, I would be offending you if I made the least recommendation in that regard. One does not need to warn the ermine against sullying his coat, nor a Christian against directly offending his God, one of the blackest of mortal sins.

I will touch briefly on the topic of temptations: women, drink, cards, etc. As I know you, you are above those disorders, and you have in your soul too proud affections to alarm me much on this head. As for drinking, I will say only one word, to put you on the defense against the camaraderies of the bar, against the hygienic "drops" at morning, digestives at midday, and aperitifs at 5, by whatever names they present themselves, "cognac" or "bitter" taken with such good comrades whose stomachs, solid or not, encourage one toward slippery joys. And I will repeat for you here what I told you before touching on human respect: the less the apparent danger, the greater the need to take precautions. A small glass of brandy, a bland but inoffensive recreation, invites a second that warms you, and a third that excites you; the fourth habituates you, and from there the man is done for, by what catastrophes! Obviously, I am putting things in their worst possible light and using the most serious examples, but not the least frequent, to make you more prudent. Clearly, one can accept an invitation, or accept it while staying "within the proper limits," but always remember to stay within them, and that is not easy. Make a strict rule for yourself, and place it under God's protection. That is called wisdom.

The other question, you resolved it in part yourself, a year ago. Your falling into circumstances where it was so difficult to triumph, your immediate repentance, the frankness and nobility of your opening up to me, your docility to my counsels, and your joy to return to God via sacramental ways, *specs unica*, all those proofs of strength, all those lessons, they keep you safe from the traps of the garrison: but here even, what prudence, what care you must take in what you see! The least relaxation of vigilance would let everything affect the blood, and you know that that is, along with murder and the oppression of the poor, the most hateful thing to God, and that genre of disorder is, when you reflect on it, an attempt, humanly and socially speaking, both atrocious and cruel. A daily prayer said to Mary, in especial view of that danger, will help you avoid the occasions, and surmount the sad transports of the flesh.

Your official duties are quite simple for a Christian: obedience, punctuality, contempt of death or suffering, when there is the occasion for it. At other times, I would recommend that you love your new profession, the most beautiful of all, second only to the vocation of the clergy and the function of the magistrate.

Today, when the army is a mass of people accessible to all the winds of politics, and recent... *infractions*, in the moral sense, have just enslaved youth to the base policy of a party of adventurers, I will tell you simply: "serve your time," be patient, and, if there should be a case of sacrilegious orders or insurrectional orders against the King and his "revolted" faithful – revolt as well! Imitate the example of that Quaker who of late preferred to alienate his freedom for years rather than infringe the prescriptions of his Church by accepting to carry weapons: that man, you can be sure of it, however heretical[23] he might be, God will send him an angel rather, at his last hour, than refuse him the light and salvation. The Catholic Church, which is divine, does not have those repugnances for the noble military profession. It proclaims obedience to Caesar, and the legitimacy of wars of frontier or principles. And that is why if, in the limited course of your military career, the alternative presented itself of combatting for that detestable government against the foreigner, combat the foreigner, and die, God wills it, for France, while praying for its King... and for the conversion of sinners; – but if a generous insurrection that one must hope for and almost wait for by the Holy Spirit of the God of hosts came to make an appearance against the present-day Filth, fight for France, and die or triumph with the King, your salvation in God.

---

[23]heretical: from the Roman Catholic Church's point of view.

If you are sent against God and his ministers, flatly refuse to serve, and suffer for God. Your father will be by your side suffering and dying with you if things get to that point.

In a word, be a Frenchman, whatever happens, and a Christian above all.

Chapter 6: Today's Novelists and Religion

By today's novelists I mean those who have followed the movement begun by Balzac, and whose immediate leader is, without question, Gustave Flaubert.

To make my title even more precise, I declare to have in sight, after Flaubert, whose omnipotent influence oppresses more or less all these authors and cruelly depresses two of them: the Goncourt Brothers, who have not produced any novel since the publication of *Madame Bovary*, – M. Zola, admittedly, and staunchly a disciple, – M. Alphonse Daudet, *naïve* plagiarist with a small, sharp jab of mawkish originality, – and finally M. Jules Vallès, almost off on his own, but marked by the initial brand, like a convict in the old days, grumbling and outraged, but marked.

I begin by acknowledging that I find much talent in these Gentlemen – with the exception of M. Daudet, – and I will explain why this brutality with respect to this "exquisite" person of the profession. To Balzac's tremendous and implacable observation, which they manage, scalpel and poignard in hand, each according to his strength and temperament, they join style, that *desideratum* of the Master's work, the style that he arduously sought after, that he almost possessed, but that always escaped him, leaving him holding merely the rich tatters of it. Correctness, solidity, poetry, the picturesque and the profound trait, that sought-after sobriety, superabundance where needed, proportion even, balance in the phrase and roundness in the period, they have all that, these gentlemen, they have it after much pain, meritoriously conquered, and after having divvied up the spoils amongst themselves more or less equally, – except, again, for that same M. Daudet, whom I seem to have it in for, but who gets on my nerves too much, me personally, so that I might be mistaken with respect to him, somewhat in spite of everyone used to being right all the time.

I will examine their work then, but only from the one point of view that interests me most and which you know already: *Religion* – how they mix it into their intrigues, the prejudices that pitiably hide it from their view, their more or less good faith in this regard, to be perfectly forthcoming, the ensuing reduction of their literary honor, and the influence of their influence [sic] on today's mores which they inherit, yes, but which they certainly add to and detract from, whether consciously or not, – ungrateful task, tough job, that I need to *expedite* in good conscience, and, for the honest writer that I am, no crueler condition, soberly, succinctly, in this *Voyage* through an entire country that is mine.

I ask for the reader's patience, then, for the several concentrated and tiresome pages that are about to follow. This examination, hard to read, and harder to write, *was necessary*!

To begin with, one word of explanation on an apparent lacuna.

Among the novelists in the class of men of great talent I just mentioned, whom I will speak more about in just a minute, there are two writers I cannot include, two novelists of transcendent merit, just as talented as the others, to say the least, more original and of a totally different ilk, because they are elevated on the wings of Faith, much higher in contemporary estimation, literarily and morally. Barbey d'Aurevilly and Paul Féval are two incontestable masters, *in a league altogether different from Balzac*, and it is fitting for me to salute them both with a word of ardent homage on the threshold of a study of admirable talents deplorably executed. Gallic spirit and French verve, good humor, and cordial ferocity are united with all the other qualities that the first group have, decupled, centupled by the sincere, militant, valiant, and heroic Catholicism that burns and blazes in their epics, which are simple like Truth, magnificent and subjugating like Truth, and beautiful.

I will place those two names, then, radiant and terrible, at the *very door*, good guardians of the terrestrial Paradise of Orthodoxy, in whose name I will examine and judge the "case" according to the conscience that God has given me, as they say in their language of reprobates, those Ancestors responsible for our still decadent decadence, the "Naturalist" novelists! (Let's employ the same term those Adams of naturalism themselves use in their proper bestiality.)

I have insisted on the gaiety, on the Gallic spirit, on the French verve, of our two great Catholic novelists. M. Paul Féval in particular gives free range in his books to hearty, cunning laughter, very cunning, which a strong nature carries in its belly like a salutary tempest that must be expressed when the time is right. M. Barbey d'Aurevilly, himself so intemperate – (and he has good reason to be!) – like a furiously ironical critic and like a full-throated polemicist, concentrates his formidable good humor in his novels, cubes it, and does not let any of it escape by small flashes, but only in blinding visions. Now, if we compare these two novelists of ours to those who will soon occupy us, we will acknowledge that their gaiety, broad or deep, is the greatest difference that could separate them, morally, from their contemporaries, colleagues, people speaking their same language in terms of education and vocation. That difference is a new honor, among all the rest, for Catholicism, which leaves to men all their faculties, all of them, on the condition that they remain true to themselves, as best they can; meanwhile, the "Naturalists," steeped, in their imagination, in vice or its morosity, it goes without saying that they cannot, must not, initially, in spite of their temperament as Frenchmen – (but they betray its tradition by adopting, with little pride, the modern laxity and anxiety, whence their ill) – they cannot help giving vent to the immense sadness that Lucretius speaks of, from experience...

In effect, the characteristic of the their work is, generally speaking, – in spite of all the very interesting qualities that I have, so willingly and so readily, conceded to them just now – of an intense morosity, a thick and heavy melancholy, and, for the reader, a leaden tedium. They all have wit but cannot express it, some have gaiety – even M. Daudet, who however does not know how to manage his – and they are incapable of laughing "a smidgen," or even of smiling. They are hungry, with a ferocity, but they lack the strength to bite, oh at all! Their comicalness, very sparse in the desolate world of their fables, is really poor.

M. Flaubert, – when he depicted Homais in his Greek cap with his two or three expressions in the style of Paul Bert, or when he made the god Crépitus "speak," and had Pécuchet completely naked and at fisticuffs with a dog temerariously suspected of hydrophobia, – is at the end of his rope.

M. Zola has nothing at all in all his baggage of the truly, cordially amusing, except Coupeau's wedding party promenading through the museum of the Louvre;[24] flip through all the rest of his books, you will find nothing, absolutely nothing, except maybe, and still! (and that is really everything!) La Faloise (in *Nana*), a sympathetic type by dint of utter stupidity and inoffensive idiocy.

The Goncourt Brothers are flat-out lugubrious, despite all the *élan* of their talent and the exquisite spontaneous impulse of their expressed sensations.

---

[24]"Coupeau...: a reference to a character and a scene at the beginning of *l'Assommoir*.

I will not talk about M. Daudet, nor about his *Tartareigne de Tarascongne*, an encumbering cock--and-bull tale with the pretext merely of striving to make the French meridionals of M. Daudet's same latitude laugh, *nobody but* them, of that same latitude; nor will I talk about his "humor" borrowed from Dickens (and how dishonored!); nor about his rather poisoned malice, to be honest, with an intent to aggrieve the weak and vanquished, but not definitive enough to remain literary.

M. Vallès, that guy, strikes a gay note, ferociously gay, the "bad guy" note, not like Villon the Great, but like Hégésippe Moreau, with the (redemptive!) hatred of Béranger and his sincere bitterness to boot. His comicalness which can get really Funny, in the absolute sense of comedy, Ludicrousness, a stand-in for dead-pan humor and Sterne[25], not imitated but congeneric, in a beautiful and fine way, triggering Rabelasian outbursts of laughter whose comical insistence and redundancy make Molière seem so full of lumbering simplicity and almost primitive. But again, sad to say, the gaiety is sad; it mocks but does not laugh for the sake of laughing; it is about others and about itself and not about their or his vices that the author makes those beautiful throats warm and causes those frank outbursts of laughter: grimace and dissonance too often alternate in those expansions, always bitter however, and sometimes spiteful, to be honest.

And for the great mass of their work, in those four or five gentlemen, first talents in prose, – less

---

[25]Sterne: Laurence Sterne (AD 1713-1768), British author, most famous for his *The Life and Opinions of Tristram Shandy*.

one, of course! – about their contemporaneous nation, what a density of horrible sadness, disillusioned but impenitent, and, to be precise, while I am wrapping things up, what a lack of religion! what an "invincible ignorance"! since then, what boredom for them (contagious to reading!) to live through characters they don't possess the key to, the bulls of Phalaris ravenous for talent, genius, literary life even, across the terrifyingly-consumed brain in that atheistic night!

Invincible ignorance, I said, but not the innocence of heretics or abandoned schismatics, or savages without missions! No, born in the Church, raised by it, at least to a certain age, in the knowledge of its precepts and counsels, possessing, more than their fellow citizens (they also, for the most part, indifferent or hostile by ignorance), an awakened intelligence and studying ancient and modern letters in order to protect them from the exceptional thickness of that already so crass ignorance, they are guilty and prevaricate even, intellectually speaking – alas! that they were not like and did not act like that! – to remain thus in the refusal of an examination of conscience and in the entirely insufficient *petitio principii* and infatuated by an indolent negation. Yes, guilty they are, they break their promise to themselves made on the day that they felt themselves to be (at least five of them) great writers of the order of Observers. Their vocation was complex, and alongside the Art that is implacable to serve, it proposed to them the strictest obedience to the most minute Inquest *into everything* and *everywhere*. Now, a rapid foray into the part played by Religion in the entirety of their writings, taken individually, will demonstrate their error to a fault; I will call it the crime of those gentlemen, impardonable literary crime, inexcusable human error, and the most inconsistent as well as the least able to be forgotten of all the ridicules coming from their writing desk!

The greater part of those gentlemen have spoken at length about Religion and priests, without knowing anything about it or them, without having seriously wanted anything to do with the one or the other. Nonetheless, as they did not insult, as they have merely profaned, a Christian writer can without bitterness, and I rejoice to say it, address the subject of their preoccupation in that regard.

Let's begin with M. Flaubert, the undisputed master of them all. He tackled the religious question in two novels primarily: *Madame Bovary* and *Bouvard et Pécuchet*. I will not speak about *Salammbô*, a very fine thing, horribly sad and furiously opaque despite all the amber, jasper, opal, and jade therein traversed, penetrated, liquified or burned by the esoteric Moon which creates all the mystery of that cruel poem. Nor will I speak about *The Temptation of Saint Anthony* (a masterpiece, however) and its feeble ironies, in a small man's loud voice, of his encounter with Biblical "Elohims" and "Jehovahs," the God of us Christians, not to mention Jews and even Deists of today and Muhammadans, people without possible polemic, but serious. Let's stick to the attack, – for without any great malice, which so distinguished a mind would have held in horror, without any really fine nastiness either, but rather in the manner of a game played by an erudite skeptic, Flaubert attacks, even while discerning every superiority... obvious to the man of Christ, and to Christ himself finally, and to his followers.

It is in this way that, in his lack of refinement, the curate Bournisien in *Madame Bovary* is *quite right*, he is always right, – right in his colloquies with Homais, which are repeated and expanded upon to such thick tedium in *Bouvard et Pécuchet* between Bouvard and the abbot Jeufroy under an umbrella held by the four hands of the interlocutors surprised by the storm, – right to send Mme. Bovary back to her husband the doctor, as that woman does not complain to him except amphibologically and does not speak quite candidly to him, at the time of her vague religious impulsions, when she desires to confess herself; – right when boxing the ears of the ragamuffins of the catechism; – right when he shuts the trap of that insufferable apothecary with a resounding "but goodness gracious!"; – right always, right everywhere, right in everything and for everything! It's the same for the curate in *Bouvard et Pécuchet,* even though the habitual irony, one would wish to believe, wanted to get mixed up with the good humor in full display on certain excellent pages, and to spoil them while spoiling it.

The abbot Jeufroy, like the abbot Bournisien, is not favored by the author in the intelligence department or that of zeal, far from it. He is a mediocre man in every possible way, weak, socially speaking, to the

extent of exhibiting "some pretension," – given he is
ordinarily simple, it is to be noted, – in the religious
instructions he gives to two poor children, "because
the audience" is composed of several people from the
village, as would be expected. Nevertheless, in the
lengthy discussions that he has the good nature to sus-
tain with the two imbecilic masters who give their
name to that review *in charge* of contemporary
French stupidity, he does not let any word escape that
is really awkward or prejudiciable to the cause that he
defends, nor does he commit a single inconsequence
of behavior in the midst of all that absurdity in action
when he debates with the numerous puppets moved
by the enormous fantasy of that grim scoffer who is
Flaubert in that unfortunately unfinished book. Finally, there is not, in all that work by the greatest novelist of the Second Empire, anything of positive blasphemy, nor even of premeditated negation. So one
cannot say that the author of *Madame Bovary* and
Bouvard et Pécuchet is fundamentally hostile to the
clergy or religion; but he introduces them into inap-
propriate situations, with the least possible respect
that is their due, by a writer of such worth who has
some self-respect, – he introduces, I say, Religion and
its ministers, like the first element of satirical observation to come along, into the examination he claims
to make on the ridiculousness, abuses, and biases of
our epoch.

Artist and stylist first and foremost, everything that is not art and style does not exist for him, or
is null and void for him; everything for him is stupid,
odious, or at minimum pointless, encumbering,
puerilely tyrannical, private virtues, the Public thing,

the fatherland, the afterlife, alas! also. With respect to
Religion, of course, its harmonies will charm him. (It
is said that he was enthralled by Chateaubriand and
incessantly re-read him! His *Genius of Christianity*
must have enthused his early childhood and had a
hand in his youth, and even in his ripe old age, becoming more and more the rhetor as time went on.)
He will consider dogmas, rituals, general precepts, the
great outlines of Christianity with the satisfied eyes of
a lover of perfect order and intellectual omnipotence;
but the humble side, the truly most beautiful side,
even from the point of view of supreme art and poetry, the practical, down-to-earth side, the conduct both
irreproachable and conciliating at the same time, the
very delicate relationship of charity with so wicked a
world, all the immense knowledge of infinitely small
details about Christianity will escape him, by every
necessity. Catechism as well, unfortunately for the
loftiness of his intelligence, Catechism, misunder-
stood, mocked, dragged into the catch-tunes of the
workshop and conversations around the table, will in
turn elude that imprudent mind, it will leave that
memory cram-full of so many vanities, and, the sun
of evidence will no longer succeed in striking those
pupils except ironically, pupils burnt by the filthy
glimmers of the flesh and the world, and which will
only sense its heat, even suffer from it, without per-
ceiving the most fugitive, palest flash of its torrential,
eternal light. Also, from the point of view even of
verisimilitude and with that *observation* that his entire
literary school so prides itself on, – what pitiable
mannequins they were, Flaubert's two priests! M.
Bournisien is especially, on the strength of the *techni-*

cal term, a "failed" individual. Look at him, after he
has heard the confession of Mme. Bovary (which the
author presents to us as sincere), at the time of her
first fall and her first disillusionment. The last village
rustic, the first porter to come along from Paris (that
world rubs shoulders with the priest more or less, vol-
untarily or against its will, and knows the general way
of his habits, of his procedures in such and such a
case), not to mention that any ex-prisoner having
passed through the hands of any almoner whatsoever,
knows that the priest, above all he whose offices call
for an assiduous visitation of his penitent, follows this
latter with the eyes of his soul, surveils him, assumes
his faults as part of his own conscience, advises him
superabundantly, invests in him in some way, lays
siege to his main sin, in a word fulfills his duty as a
priest unfailingly, absolutely, integrally, because such
is his dogma, such is his discipline, and, more than
anything else, such is his faith. Now, what does Bournisien do, if no longer concerned with Mme. Bovary,
once her "devotion" has grown cold, after the danger
of death has passed, that Homais himself would not
do in his place by a totally gratuitous supposition? Let
us note moreover, in passing, that Bovary, in general
a marvelously behaved type of little woman, very
poorly raised, whose intelligence and temperament
was entrusted to the deplorable hands of a poor devil
of a husband, both good-natured and vulgar, prompt-
ing her to all the rages of even more vulgar, and so
shameful, so craven, adulteries! – let us note, I say,
that the sad but logical heroine of the best book by
Flaubert loses all her terrible and sometimes tragic reality in order to flop around like a doll, to degenerate

into a third-rate artist's caricature, as soon as the author gets it into his head to have her mixed up with things of the altar. The scene of her education in a convent is a *type accompli* of poorly-informed insincerity. Do you honestly believe, for example, in those facilities of correspondence between the pupils of the good ladies of the Ursulines and the sempiternal old high-society woman whom Victor Hugo has already yammered on about in his interminable stroll through the monstrous Petit-Picpus in the *Misérables*? – No, certainly not, no more than I do, nor Flaubert for that matter, who employed that vileness on account of laziness, and, also, I dare repeat, because of a touch of complacency for that Voltarian Prudhomme whom he professes to abhor and whom he spent his life, as a person who likes to chat, anathematizing, so we are told, without realizing that one existed in him, a thick Philistine, and not without some very bourgeois vices, who was not any less hostile to the Church, even if only instinctively, than the reflection of it in his book, in the expansive, indiscreet, compromising Homais. And then, what does he want from us with those languors at vespers by the future spouse of the far too pitiable Charles, and her unhealthily ecstatic interest in the mystery of stained glass windows, and her dreams suggestive of a sluggish street urchin for such and such a statuette of the chapel? What sort of Burgraves does he take us for by serving up that ancient nonsense? Where did he get that Catholicism of "Paphos" and Epinal? In what romance? From what Pigault-Lebrun, or off what other steaming pile of horse manure? It's really the first time, it's the only time, that a first-rate mind, excellent for the most part, very

meticulously informed, curious to a fault, could have
depicted the offices so perfectly *right* out of the
Church, – the symbols, so neat and of so clear an instruction, of always so simple and so sane a decora-
tion in its marvelous poetry of all our sanctuaries
without exception, – as the vague and nebulous vehi-
cle, in some sort, of languishing fancies, indolent reli-
giosities, *superficial* and nothing but *superficial* mysticism, pestilential baggage and rotten conductors,
forerunners, and harbingers of impure Vice incarnate!
What ineptitude and sacrilege!

As for the religious crisis, the "conversion" of
Bouvard and of Pécuchet, that passage from a book
with such great ironic pretensions is decidedly feebler
than any other in the world. I was speaking earlier of
the squalid Pigault-Lebrun who had at least, with
some grammar, a bit of spirit, although quite contemptible. Here we must, in order to express the extreme platitude of that caricature, descend to the level
of an evocation of Paul de Kock, – it brings so much
bad luck to oneself to touch on religion with one's
hands still feverish and dirty from all the literary,
artistic, and philosophical tasks of the century! As I
have already said, there is in that episode, several gay
pages, a good bit of satire, heavy and profound, but
that a spiteful laugh Voltarianizes, so to speak, makes
acidic, adds saltpeter to, renders as displeasant as possible. Then, M. Jeufroy would yield points to M.
Bournisien in his capacity as a weak polemicist. Hear
me out – on the strength of things, and by the influence of something great, instinctively endured by
Gustave Flaubert's fundamentally generous and expansive mind, rather than by a well-reflecting will on

his part, *as the author*, – those two mediocre priests
never yield, having never been wrong with respect to
their opponents, who are otherwise so miserable? No,
but they fall too far below the mark of down-to-earth
mediocrity and self-conceit which the author has created an atmosphere of in his modern novels, so as not
to participate, let's be honest, in the ambient stupidity, and both their polemics suffer for it. It is in this
way, citing only one example, that a needled abbot
Jeufroy (that's the only *mot juste*, taken in the most
literal acceptation of the expression), needled, I say,
by one of the two grotesques, straightforward and
vividly portrayed, one has to admit it, by Flaubert in
his posthumous novel, on the subject of the Holy
Trinity, – that a needled abbot who has in hand and
by rote, like *any other* priest, to be sure, the most luminous and decisive responses possible, those of elementary theology, – it is in this way that he extricates
himself via circular arguments and lame comparisons
which a freshman seminarist, what am I saying, a
child of catechism from my village, would have been
ashamed of!... One last grievance, not the least, to
conclude with Flaubert, in his relationship as a writer
with the Church, it is the manner in which, on two
different occasions, among the other more or less sincere nonsense, he speaks of Saint Teresa! One does
not avenge Saint Teresa any more than one avenges
the Catholic Church, but it is not permissible for a
Christian holding a quill and encountering such lamentable things to let them pass without condemning
them by immediate and complete citation... "Instead
of the sublimities that he expected (Pécuchet), he will
encounter only platitudes, a very lax style, frigid im-

ages and forced comparisons, drawn from the lap-
idary shops..." (*Bouvard et Pécuchet*, Lemerre publisher, page 321)... "Salammbô is a maniac, a kind of
Saint Teresa..." (Letter by Gustave Flaubert to Sainte-
Beuve, dated December 1862, published in the appen-
dix of the definitive edition of *Salammbô*, G. Charp-
entier publisher, 1877). – There is no way he could
have read a single chapter written by Saint Teresa and
say such a thing: Saint Teresa, the subtle dialectics
and penetrating psychology *par excellence*, expressed
in the most vivid, rapid, clear, and most soberly and
distinctly descriptive of styles! And he must have
never read about her in the most abridged of bio-
graphical dictionaries, to utter the word, otherwise
coarse and stupid, of "maniac," precisely with respect
to that marvelous activity, unique perhaps in the history of minds, perpetually at attention in all lofty di-
rections, contemplation, administration, politics, –
one is familiar with her magnificent correspondence
with Philippe II, – literature finally, and I intend by
that word the entirety of operations of a mind that
wants to express the most conscientiously, the most
exactly, the most intimately possible, what it senses
that God suggests to it of strong, great, loving things,
for the advancement and edification of one's neighbor. One needs to deplore, and bitterly deplore, these
faults in Flaubert,[26] and most particularly the last out-

---

[26]Original footnote: All that is left for me to do is note down an
ugly jest made against the *Catechism of Perseverance* by Mgr.
Gaume, that learned and instructive *compendium* whose luminous unction knew how to penetrate so many hearts, and the logic
of so many minds. The author of the present work holds, for his
part, an infinite gratitude for that modest and excellent book,
wherein he found, in the first moments of a slow but sure return
to the Faith, so much intellectual succor and consolation. It would

rage, which was without thinking, so be it! but very serious and scandalous to the Holy Spirit, to compare at the same time, for one second, little things with great things, – what an impardonable breach of the most elementary laws of justice and literary taste![27]

I have laid quite a bit into Flaubert, the leader of the new school of novelists, seeing that we are still up to our ears in schools to the point of anarchy and our un-raveling, politically speaking and otherwise! This at-tention that I had to pay, to be as minutely detailed as possible in the first part of the present examination, will free me from dwelling for so long on the other writers of fiction aimed at in this chapter.

MM. Zola and the Brothers Goncourt have spoken much more than Flaubert about Priests and Religion. M. Zola has consecrated, for his part, two thick vol-umes to the recitation of actions and deeds of priests, independently of all ecclesiastics and the "devout," whom he makes intervene in the entirety of his work. *La faute de l'abbé Mouret* attempts to show us a young village curate, tempted, succumbing, recover-ing, – good, naïve, saintly also, as can be imagined and traced out for us by the coarse temperament and fundamentally bawdy – pardon the word – mind of

be, moreover, anyone's guess whether Flaubert even *opened* that book or others!

[27]Footnote on the previous footnote: See the preface, and also see *My Prisons* (*Mes Prisons*) by Verlaine, wherein he mentions Mgr. Gaume and his *Catechism*.

that author of a very real but very corrupt talent, with all the excellent beauty that remains of a robust health smashed to pieces by every clumsy excess *in extremis* and indiscretion. *La conquête de Plassans* is the story of a priest of a certain age already, ambitious, tenacious, proud, atrocious finally, and fierce in his pursuit of the domination first of a family, then of an entire town. That last novel swarms with grotesqueries, not only relative to the abbot Faujas, – a type of Eugène Sue (and what a shame for a writer of M. Emile Zola's stature, very honest fundamentally, let's keep in mind) – but also concerning his principal "victim," a lady Mouret who falls from absolute indifference in matters of religion into the excesses of "devotion" and of "mysticism" such as Naturalist novelists conceive of, those slaves, to hear them speak, of the literal fact and the authentic "document." In it, it is only a matter of "the delights of paradise," of "tender feeling, of unstoppable tears... that that lady shed without feeling them fall"! of the nervous crises that she came out of, weakened, fainting. "She has fits of shouting and nocturnal catalepsies after each religious ceremony," etc., etc., which did not stop her from growing more embittered with each passing day, of becoming querulous, *fussy*, what do I know? O simplicity of Faith, calmness of Charity, fresh assurance and firm discretion of eternal Hopes, whoever has known you once or simply suspected you, and caught a glimpse of you elsewhere, – must he laugh or weep for such scenes? What ignorance of you, just heaven! and what an abortion of such gross pretensions to analyze you in such great detail, exactly as those gentlemen are in the habit of doing, dissecting, so well this time,

the dirty ambitions, the sad lusts, the ignoble jeal-
ousies of a world they practice and frequent, at minimum! *La faute de l'abbé Mouret*, (the abbot Mouret,
by the way, is the son of Mme. Mouret in *La conquête de Plassans* – M. Zola has some ideas on men-
tal and psychological heredity and a "scientific" system for speaking its language when he acts the child,
which he puts into circulation quite disagreeably and
quite in vain in his books), *La faute de l'abbé Mouret*,
I say, contains – with the horrors of obscenity and
against commonsense, – some beautiful things, some
interesting developments, and some admirable de-
scriptions in certain places; but as the author is mistaken as soon as he wishes to enter into the mind of
his hero, "into the skin of his bloke," as people say
these days! I do not want to call out, nor can I, all the
errors and all the monstruosity of errors into which
M. Zola, the psychologist of a Catholic priest, falls;
but all the same the saddest errors among them will
be at least pointed out in these cursory pages. Imagine
this, that the abbot, having just exited Zola's brain,
armed to the hilt with sanctity, with doctrine, etc.,
sees in the Holy Virgin Mary "a woman," a sister, a
kind of fiancée, worse still (unconsciously, innocent-
ly, if I dare say so), finally he is afraid of her, leaves
his particular cult, him who is so learned and pious!
because of the MOTHER, the *queen*, and the special
female advocate of the Clergy!

Let's see, what Catholic will be made to believe in the probability of such a conception, of such
an evolution in the soul of a priest who is presented
by the author as being absolutely correct insofar as
orthodox? And would it not be pitiful to see a man

like Zola stumble so pathetically on such material, on *that* material to be precise, – O revenge of logic and vengeance of sacred Truth! – was not the holy sanctuary impenetrable to the skepticism even of talent and genius, – of sacerdotal conscience, such as the Universal Roman investiture made it?

I abridge this review [of M. Zola], and I arrive now at the Brothers Goncourt, who have, in *Madame Gervaisais*, consecrated all the effort of their exquisite and cruel talent for description – such is the *mot juste* for those patient, albeit nervous, artists of the quill, I was going to say of the "burin," – of a very strange conversion and of a very theatrical death, and quite *chic* for a "saint" of such lofty taste. A lady again, this one, one of the most distinguished, who, seduced by the beauties of the Catholic cult seen in Rome, passes from the poly-technical pedanticism of a modern-day Mme. Roland, – without the politics however, – to mystical ambitions that smack a little of their very dark bluestockings. She changes confessors for lack of enough severity in their direction, imposes ferocious penances on herself by her own authority, takes up a series of prayers fit more for a fakir or a Quaker, but assuredly not for a Catholic, and from there it is not surprising that, having passed all her life as a "convert" – several months! – doing the exact opposite of what a simple, confident, and humble believer would do, she almost apostatizes in the end under the pressure of a gendarme brother, in order, without transition, to die finally for joy, and... apoplexy, because she sees the Pope in a scheduled Papal audience!!! I repeat, how similar absurdities dishonor an [otherwise] illustrious literature, and what a shame it would be if God did not get something out of it in demonstration of the efficacy of the one Faith, and of the one *sancta simplicitas* for the knowledge of sacred things!

I like M. Vallès quite a bit, and I find him very sweet and very exquisite in spite of his sometimes insufferable childishness and the potshots he takes straight into the reader's face. He also has a bit of Paul de Kock in him, but not like Flaubert who took from Homer the blue ribbons of heaviness and stupidity only; no, M. Vallès has very legitimately borrowed, like a man who takes back his own whenever he finds it, the quick, direct, and present-tense narrative, the naïve and spontaneous drollery, with, what is more, and without taking into account, of course, correctness and style, happy finds that are as amusing as anything, violent and gay bursts of color, whirlings, sparkles, and furious visions in charcoal, in the manner of Dickens. But then, at least, M. Vallès does not practice theology. He declares himself, or rather he shows himself to be hostile to all that presently exists, Universality (and he is quite right!), family (and he would be wrong if it was not a question of the family such as 1789 has given us!), republicans whom he has known, himself a skeptical and naïve republican, those he sees, disgusted by them, and those whom his nausea anticipates, etc., etc. How would the clergy escape the animadversion of that disrespectful man of instinct? Even here, despite everything, by the appli-

cation of Logic, there is *instinctive respect*, – might I
say at least partial sympathy? It is thus that Jacques
Vingtras has an uncle who is a curate, depicted as an
excellent man, – the best, the *finest* character in the
book *l'Enfant*; but as bad luck would have it that uncle receives his colleagues at supper, and it is then
that M. Vallès speaks to us about venomous gossip,
spitefulness behind people's back; then the carica-
tures, "dirty rabats," "serpent heads," an "old man
who looks drunk," all the crude phantasmagoria of
the Charlets from the bottom-shelf, of the decadent
Goyas... I declare that I have had, me a layperson,
very laically raised, in these last five or six years, the
very great honor and pleasure of living with priests of
all ages, on a footing of great intimacy, and that I
have never observed among them scandalmongering
or even gossip: good humor and some rather anodyne
mischievousness, at most one or two vivacious outbursts quickly repressed, but that's it. Besides, the life
of priests, their rule, their long apprenticeship at the
seminary in all the virtues and all the qualities, the *esprit* finally that *they partake of*, preserved them from
every vice of a primary school education or rectified
every acquired penchant too vulgarly blamable. I
don't do honor to the other "objections" indicated by
concerning myself with them, other than by feeling
sincerely sorry for the author, who is so far above
them, and whom the century's idiocy debases on this
lamentable occasion. But how very particularly unjust
the world is to attribute its troubles and its excuses to
those who, by choice, do not live in it!

There is also that instance, in *The Baccalaure-
ate*, a... an inexactitude that it is important not to

overlook. I would gladly cite the page, which is
charming, and it is in Vallès' best style, if it weren't
for the spirit of insult that is decidedly too low and
which dishonors it. I will summarize it briefly. It has
to do with a manifestation of student-republicans,
"troubled" by the police whom young men belonging
to the Society of Saint-Vincent de Paul applaud in
bad taste. Agitation of the manifestants. The students
and the "Saint-Vincents" come to blows. Jacques, the
hero of the novel, – a thinly-veiled autobiography –
falls on one of those he heard and saw cry "bravo!"
and, holding him by the ear, forces him to swear that
he didn't see anything; then, after having let him go,
reflects a little, grabs him again, and administers a
kick *somewhere*, without any further resistance on the
part of the young man as if that last person was the
last among... *cowards*, because a "Saint-Vincent."
The author makes it quite clear what we should think.
Eh well, M. Vallès was a victim, then, not of a bad
memory, but of the stupidest French prejudice of
1789 which he subscribed to, as a man of wit, a man
of right thinking, in rebellion against all the bourgeois
stupidities, and 1789 is as bourgeois in an atrocious
way as it is atrocious in a bourgeois way. That prejudice suggests that to be a Christian one does not have
hands at the end of one's arms, nor feet at the end of
one's legs in certain circumstances. Worldly men,
who never tire of their mockery of the Gospel's doctrine of turning the other cheek, the true meaning of
which, moreover, they don't understand and who
scoff at the Saints when they practiced this divine
precept literally, are always stupefied to see that
Christians, like others, and often better than others,

hit hard, when they have to, at rascals and wiseguys who pick a fight with them for no reason, their being reputedly defenseless. From there, it is just one step to concluding that, in general, a "devotee" is nothing more than a hypocrite hiding behind grimaces and a primordial cowardice under stock expressions; and M. Vallès is mistaken to give himself away lamentably, mark my words, after having presented to us his "Saint-Vincent" like a perturber of perturbers in the street, an applauder of the police (quite plausible in this particular instance as in five out of six cases, moreover), like a rowdy himself consequently and a resolute disturber of the peace, and a bravo, only then to turn around and present that fellow to us like a "quitter" or loser of the type exhibited, just the opposite, daily, with his loud howlers and the demonstratives at a distance from the universal *Marianne,* as much his own as Vallès', the blood red like bulls and "nosebleeds" which the R. F. of potbellies and ruffians, whom he so justly hates and despises and who give it to him, duly authorized, – politically speaking, of course, for M. Vallès!

I'm going to have to stop here, regretfully; I would have loved to continue pursuing a writer I so much appreciate, – if only to prove to him incidentally just how wrong he is to detest Greek and Latin studies, progenitors of his correct, fine, and amazing talent, never tangled up in the ignorant rhetoric of our descriptor-painters. But such a digression and yet others that tempt me, would lead me too far afield for this book, and I am forced to conclude this study after one word or two, alas! on the sad M. Daudet.

M. Alphonse Daudet is one of the greatest objections I have against the French *Midi*.

Nobody more than I lavishes praise on the extreme intelligence, lively perception, natural eloquence of our meridionals; unfortunately, all that is not consistent: splendid rough outlines, great beginnings, – then nothing; the work always aborts in their ardent hands, they are unparalleled *bunglers*: in politics as in everything else, they are always the Girondins of the thing; much weakness with a lot more noise; as well, the encumbrances that they are and that they cause are most particularly displeasing; one sees only their hands gesticulating, one hears only their "assent," everywhere, always, and they always speak incorrectly, and they wiggle their way out of everything! Some of them are really great and kind, Mistral, the felibres (the real ones), those who stay put when the hunger for places and the thirst for vainglory does not send them running, grinding their teeth and sticking their tongue out, from the proud poverty of their ancestors..., but the "zothers," but the most famous among them, it is Alphonse Daudet! Now, if ever there was a bungler and a failed wit, it is he, it is that poet of the "plums," an ineptness stupider still than the salons where he made his fortune, that storyteller, that muddier of people's back, that man who churns out artificially precious little articles on too true banalities, the foreshortened, the mawkish hunchback with pretty airs, – suddenly standing up straight, gangling, warped in that diffuse novelist, puerily anecdotal, with a language plagiarized from everywhere, and laden with all the borrowings, without any firmness of unity. His vocation was to remain episodic, a fragmenteer, an essayist of small flights, something like a shrill Xavier de Maistre, and look at him now: swollen to the size of a Balzac in order to laugh! Is that not the most abominable abortion of his talent, as a venomous *cigalier* and a piercing cicada with the harsh but vibrant cry, and not without a naughty grace; as that sudden, coarse, impudent, shameless plagiarist; as that sudden, impudent, and dishonest imitator of Flaubert and others of his same ilk; of their style, their tics..., their ideas, hig-gledy-piggledy, one after the other, *grosso modo*, without the least respect for himself or the reader, – ah, the reader! But let's pass over to the absolute lack of merit, in my eyes, of M. Alphonse Daudet, so pop-ular – and that is natural – with the lugubriously cretinous public that we have today, such a *comrade* among literatasters, and it makes sense, given he is so influential in bookstores – and let's finish with that "sign of the times," by denouncing once again (for one begins to pull off the mask of that falsely honest man of letters) the hateful political and social system of the exobligated, of the Empire's sycophant, turned nauseatingly republican, a system of injurious depre-ciation of the past and of the present if it is feeble, a system of walking all over the dead and with insult to the persecuted and vanquished, – but what is exquisitely vengeful in the case of that apostate and repudiator of the vanquished, is this: that in his ardor to please his patrons of the hour, the pampered and pampering ruffians that one knows, he too, poor little imprudent man, he has an axe to grind with the Good God and the Church; he spits on the latter in the per-son of an archbishop martyr (vid. *le Nabab*) and on the Almighty and All-Bountiful in the form of a really hateful attack on prayer and on those who pray finally (*Numa Roumestan*), after the example of his older brothers in "Naturalism," those infinitely superior masters in talent and character (who have never flattered and do not flatter any regime, nor any prejudice, except the anti-religious one, but that is instinctive, and in the blood, alas!) he puts the last blasphemy, the supreme curse, into the mouth of his characters, he saturates his pages with it, he revels in it, one would think. All of it, note well, villainy, palinody, impiety, without conviction (under the Empire, he *put out* poor-quality stuff in religiosity and in monarchism) without anything of any sort of any minor plausibility, uniquely through imitation of speculation, or speculation of imitation, for everything is topsy-turvy here, reputation, talent, conditions of success or failure, and it is the least talented person, without any sort of comparison possible, who sees his books *sold*, – for it is the low-water mark of modern-day literature, – no longer by the edition, that's too old school! but by the "thousands," like straw!

I have spoken, in all honesty, at too great a length about so very poor a subject, and I generalize my preceding remarks: whoever has read these gentlemen knows the French spirit, I mean the entire French spirit, and by that I intend the French spirit outside the Church (I will speak later about him who has stayed within the Church, the true Church!), the official French spirit, which is boisterous, which sets the example, – and, isn't that right that, thanks to that ignorance of the Catechism, which I noted in my first chapters, isn't that right that from Voltaire to Thiers and from Thiers to... this, that we have fallen so low, like the bourgeoisie, because our authors are the bourgeoisie of education and fortune, they are, whatever they might possess, – talent aside, fundamentally – and I cannot say it often enough on account of the total disregard for the small Catechism, MM. Zola, Flaubert, Vallès, the Brothers Goncourt even, better bred and elevated, it is Prudhomme and it is Homais, and it is intellectually much less than that, if that's even possible!

M. Daudet, himself, does not exist... happily!

I have not mentioned anything about the horrible lust that the overall corpus of these masters abounds in and overflows with, any more than the colossal tiresomeness that is inseparable from that saddest of sins. It is the double chastisement both of a like literature and the readers who feed on it. But all the same, what a fine and great talent is dishonored, lost, – to be detested like the plague and even worse!

Other Books by the Publisher

Fanchette's Pretty Little Foot by Restif de La Bretonne

Je M'Accuse... by Léon Bloy

My Hospitals & My Prisons by Paul Verlaine

Salvation Through the Jews by Léon Bloy

Words of a Demolitions Contractor by Léon Bloy

Cellulely by Paul Verlaine

Ecclesiastical Laurels by Jacques Rochette de la Morlière

Flowers of Bitumen by Émile Goudeau

Songs for Her & Odes in Her Honor by Paul Verlaine

On Huysmans' Tomb by Léon Bloy

Ten Years a Bohemian by Émile Goudeau

The Soul of Napoleon by Léon Bloy

Blood of the Poor by Léon Bloy

Theresa the Philosopher & The Carmelite Extern Nun by Marquis d'Argens & Anne-Gabriel Meusnier de Querlon

A Platonic Love by Paul Alexis

Two Novellas: Francine Cloarec's Funeral and Benjamin Rozes by Léon Hennique

The Revealer of the Globe: Christopher Columbus & His Future Beatification (Part One) by Léon Bloy

Joan of Arc and Germany by Léon Bloy

Héloïse Pajadou's Calvary by Lucien Descaves

An Immodest Proposal by Dr. Helmut Schleppend

The Pornographer by Restif de La Bretonne

Style (Theory and History) by Ernest Hello

On the Threshold of the Apocalypse: 1913-1915 by Léon Bloy

She Who Weeps (Our Lady of La Salette) by Léon Bloy

The Sylph by Claude Prosper Jolyot de Crébillon (*fils*)

School of Woman by Nicolas Chorier

www.ingramcontent.com/pod-product-compliance
Lightning Source LLC
Chambersburg PA
CBHW031445120626
46545CB00006B/2566